ENJOY THE BOOK

Steven E. Daniel

ONE SOLDIER'S MEMORIES

WORLD WAR II

By

STEVEN E. DANISH

ONE SOLDIER'S MEMORIES

WORLD WAR II

By

STEVEN E. DANISH

GREENE PUBLICATIONS, INC.
Island Park, New York
(516) 897-7224
http://www.greenepublicationsinc.com

Cover Design by Steven E. Danish

Cover illustrations by Stacy Sideris

Photographs by Len Totora, Jr. / L&L Camera, Inc.

ACKNOWLEDGMENTS

First I must thank my dearest friend, and loving wife for her invaluable assistance, insight, support and patience in my undertaking of this sizable project.

I thank my father, for without him, there would be no story.

My special thanks to Alan L. Kessler, Kathleen Gladstone, Jim Davis and to all the other people who gave me their support and encouragement.

Above all, I am grateful to the soldiers of the Allied Forces who sacrificed their lives to keep our country free.

FOREWORD

My father was a hard working man, an average guy. Over fifty years ago he was a soldier in the army, a Private First Class in the 1285th Engineer Combat Battalion, H & S Company. He fought in the European theater and served his country a total of three years, one month and six days. Armed with faith, determination and a bit of luck, he survived the insanity. Coming home a decorated soldier, he bore scars that could not be seen and endured experiences and made sacrifices of which no one was aware. His powerfully graphic and fascinating story is as filled with torment as it is with triumph and humor. It is an indispensable record for posterity. A little piece of history put down on paper, that unlike the man, will live on forever.

CONTENTS

Acknowledgments

Foreword

Chapter 1
Before the War

My name is Jacob Danish. My friends know me as Jack. I was seventeen and a half years old and had already graduated from Stuyvesant High School which was located in Manhattan. I was living with my parents and sister in an apartment house in the Bronx on the corner of Burnside and University Avenues.

Sunday, December 7, 1941, was a clear, crisp day. I walked down University Avenue that afternoon to go to the Loews movie theater. Its location on Tremont Avenue was where the trolley cars ran. The Loews was not the closest theater but it was the nicest. They charged a few cents more but I felt it was worth it.

Late that afternoon after the movies I returned home. No one else had gotten home yet. So far it had been an ordinary Sunday. I had no idea how radically things were about to change. Looking for something to do I turned on the radio (we didn't have television in those days). The announcer's voice sounded distressed as he reported about the massive bombing of Pearl Harbor. At that point in time I didn't even know what Pearl Harbor was. It didn't take long to find out. I was hearing how Japanese war planes had made a devastating assault on our battleships, pulverizing them into a molten blazing mass, killing many men. All of a sudden it hit me. America was at war! A surge of horror and outrage ran through my mind. I worried about the impact this brutal act would have on the nation and my life. I remember those were grim, black days.

Shaken by the invasion but too young to enlist, I went on with my life the best I could. I got a job as a machinist. I was also going to City College of New York at night and had a new girlfriend. The mood of the country was one of shock and fury at the attackers. Monumental tasks needed to be accomplished that would profoundly affect the lives of millions of people. A complex system of rationing and coupon books were being put into place. Factories that had been making civilian products were converting to wartime production.

It was a year later and the war continued. I was eighteen and a half and decided it was time to do my patriotic duty. I went down to the local draft board to enlist. I was informed I could no longer enlist. It was now a voluntary draft. To me that sounded pretty much the same, so I put my name down. A few weeks later I received notice that I was leaving on January 4, 1943 for Fort Dix, New Jersey.

Everyone scheduled to leave that day reported to the draft board. Arrangements had been made to take us by subway to Grand Central Station. Only days before departing, I became engaged to my girlfriend. We made plans to get married when the war was over. God willing, I would get home in one piece. The day before I left, I packed my suitcase with the bare minimums. My mother went with me to Grand Central Station. At the station, an ocean of men were carrying luggage and saying good-bye to loved ones. I was on my way to the induction center to start the process of getting into the army. I was feeling apprehensive about the challenges I would face, but didn't want anybody to know.

As soon as we arrived we were issued clothing and given haircuts. Boxes were given to us to mail our civilian clothing home. The army would supply us with everything we needed to wear.

Large tents that held ten men were our living quarters. It was winter and especially cold early in the morning. A lousy little pot bellied coal stove in the middle of the tent was all we had to keep us warm.

The army was now testing us. There were written tests, I.Q. tests and medical tests. They poked, prodded and injected us. You name it and they did it to us.

The testing was over and we were waiting for openings in the different basic training schools. To kill time the army had us marching around in straight lines picking up cigarette butts. This is what they called policing the area. What a treat this was!

Well, I passed muster and completed the first hurdle. I was now on my way to phase two for bigger and better things.

Chapter 2
Basic Training

Finally, after twelve stressful days at Fort Dix, I was being sent to Fort McClellan, Alabama. This is where I would receive my basic infantry training. I was assigned to the 11th Battalion, Company D. I spent hours memorizing my serial number. This was high on the army's priority list. They were going to make a soldier out of me whether I liked it or not. Walter Winchell, a reporter, had called Fort McClellan the concentration camp of the south. I had no idea what to expect, but I was sure it wouldn't be fun.

I was relieved to see I was going to be in regular army barracks, not tents. The barracks were small, low, long, one story wooden structures built off the ground on pylons so rain water wouldn't get in. I'd say they held about thirty five to forty men. Next to the bunks there was a place to hang clothing. I've never seen a place where everything was lined up in such an orderly fashion. It all looked so perfect and unused, like a display in a department store window. I would spend the next three months living at this facility.

A cadre of men consisting of officers, lieutenants, sergeants and corporals would teach us everything. Classes on military science and proper procedure were at the top of the list. I learned there was a right way, a wrong way and the army way of doing things. I learned how to hurry up and wait! This seemed to be standard army procedure. Army etiquette: I was to salute the uniform, not the man. It was just common decency to show respect to an officer. Most of the men in the cadre were old timers. Some had been in the military most of their lives. These men didn't need a uniform to look imposing. They spoke in a clear, confident tone, and did what I still say today was "the best damn job I have ever seen".

Television often portrays soldiers being yelled at while in basic training. That was not my experience. I was never subject to any type of harassment or demoralizing treatment. There was never any rousting men out in the middle of the night to march in the rain. I always knew when and where I was going to march. The kind of clothing and type of uniform to wear were posted. Everything I needed to know was always posted. Military training was rigorous enough as it was. I was thankful for the way I was being treated.

We were all teenagers, many of us away from home for the first time. Up to this point, the army was the most exciting thing that had ever happened in my life.

The magnitude of things I needed to l
staggering and exhausting, come ni
to do was go to sleep. There wasn'
about being homesick. Besides, m
boy scout camp had taken care of that. Living in a
racks with forty men for the first time certainly presented
its challenges. It was embarrassing to sit on a toilet
where everyone was able to see. Urinating in a trough in
front of dozens of guys took a little getting used to. At
first, some of the guys were unable to do this. But with
time, we all started adjusting to army life and formed
friendships.

Firing a rifle for the first time was a little scary. I
didn't know what to expect. In my class we had a group
of southern boys we used to call hillbillies. They had
been shooting rifles all their lives and bragged that they
had the proficiency to shoot the eye out of a rattlesnake.
Once I mastered the proper way to use my weapon, I
was able to out shoot any hillbilly.

1912, thirty caliber British Enfield rifles were issued. The Enfield was a bolt action, single shot, breech
loading rifle that held five bullets and weighed about eight
pounds. The cartridges were attached to a metal clip
which separated when pushed into the rifle. Each time
the rifle was fired, the bolt had to be drawn back to eject
the empty shell, then pushed forward to load the next
cartridge. The Enfield was a good reliable rifle, but not
exactly what I would call up to date. It was soon to be replaced by a more modern weapon.

Things were well organized at the rifle range. About one hundred men would be there at a time. Instructions on how the rifle worked were given first. Should a rifle jam, we needed to know how to disassemble, clean and fix it. Instructions on the different firing positions were given. We used the sitting, prone and standing positions with the rifle strap wrapped around our left arms. Resting the rifle against anything while shooting was never allowed. The range was divided into three parts: the firing line, a two hundred yard field, and a pit area at the end of the field where the targets were located. We were grouped into teams for the different jobs that needed to be done. The jobs were rifle men, firing line men, pit men, ammunition men and score keepers. Twenty men stood ready to shoot at the firing line. Standing behind them were the line men and ammunition men. Instructors called out how many shots would be fired. They called if it were to be a single or rapid fire session. Clips with the right amount of cartridges were then handed to the shooter by the ammunition men. Instructors yelled "ready on the firing line!" The next command was "lock and load!" The shooters would load the rifle, barrel always facing down field. Instructors yelled "ready on the left, ready on the right!" Line men shouted back "ready" as long as the shooters were ready. Instructors called out "commence firing!" Line men tapped the shooters on their helmets which meant start shooting. Pulling that trigger for the first time could frazzle anyone's nerves. The targets were two hundred yards away and five yards apart. They were white in color, five foot by five foot, with a black dot in the center measuring one foot in diameter and looked very small from this distance. The instructors bellowed "cease fire!" Line men tapped the shooters on their helmets again to stop firing. The shooters stood back from the firing line opening the bolts on their rifles, ejecting any unused bullets. Ammo men picked up all spent and live ammunition. Loaded clips were given to the shooters for the next round of firing. The pungent smell of burnt gunpowder permeated the air. I now knew what a rifle recoil felt like and what it sounded like to be in the midst of gunfire.

Once the shooting stopped, the pit men went to work. The pit was a deep, long, below ground area, resembling a concrete baseball dugout. It had a toilet facility and wooden benches to sit on while waiting for the shooting to stop. A dirt mound was piled up in front of the pit opening for extra protection. No one was ever in danger of being exposed to the firing.

Window sash devices were used to pull the targets both up and down. After pulling down a used target, three inch, top-shaped, wooden plugs were jammed into the holes the bullets had left. Black plugs were used in the white areas and white in the black. This was done so when the targets were raised again, everyone at the firing line could see where the targets had been hit. It only took pit men seconds to perform this job. If any of the bullets missed the target, a long wooded pole was raised. Attached to the top of the pole were a pair of red ladies underwear. It was waved back or forth to call attention to the amount of times the target was missed. This was called "flying Maggie's drawers".

Back at the firing line, the score keepers wrote down scores. Instructors scrutinized the targets for discrepancies in bullet hole patterns. If any were noticed, the problem was evaluated, instructions given and adjustments made. Shooters waited their turn to shoot again to see if the problems were alleviated.

Back at the pit, targets were pulled down again. This time, paper patches the same color as the targets were placed over the plugged holes. The targets looked new and were raised for reuse.

When it was time to leave the pit area, we exited at the far end. We always walked down the side of the field and only during a cease fire for safety reasons. There was no back stop behind the targets. The bullets would travel over a mile until they hit a tree or just fell to the ground. For obvious reasons, no one was ever allowed on the field.

My favorite job was the pit. It was easy and I had ample time to rest or read. In the summer it was cool and shady. Of course, come winter it got pretty cold in there. To break up the monotony, we used to sing a humorous song about flying Maggie's drawers. It went something like this:

The red red drawers that Maggie wore
They were nice, they were new
You could see that as they flew

They were hand stitched, they were tucked
You could see where she's been fucked
Oh those red red drawers that Maggie wore.

The word S.N.A.F.U. was used frequently around here. It meant "Situation Normal, All Fucked Up". This seemed to be standard military procedure.

I was also trained to use the B.A.R. or Browning Automatic Rifle. This was one big baby! It weighed in at about fourteen pounds and had a retractable bipod attached to the muzzle. With this rifle, I could blaze away at five hundred yards. That's quite a few city blocks. It could also be used like a fully automatic machine gun. Unlike the Enfield, this thirty caliber fed ammunition automatically from a magazine at the bottom of the rifle. This was one efficient killing machine.

Medals were given to those completing courses with high marks. They were proudly displayed from a cross that hung on the front of our uniforms. I received two for marksmanship, one for the Enfield rifle and the other for the Thompson submachine gun. Overseas, my rifle would be one means of survival. I was making sure I was proficient!

There were numerous short courses, lectures and demonstrations on a variety of weapons and equipment. A course on small cannons turned out to be a total waste of time. These cannons were so ineffective they would barely dent a German tank. Unfortunately, that's what the army had at the time. Wrestling and bayonet use were taught in case hand to hand combat was necessary. Overseas, bayonet use was limited to opening C-ration cans, at least in my company, that is. Of course, there would always be our trusty and indispensable little P-38 folding can opener. Only officers were given the course on hand guns, or side arms, as the army called them.

Learning how to carry, pack and wear our knapsacks was not fun, especially when they were poorly designed World War I issue. Blankets had to be laid out on the ground. Underclothing was placed on top and the blankets were rolled up. They were then tied to straps that hung from the back of the knapsacks. It was easy to see the problem with that design!

By this time it, was becoming obvious to all of us that the army was not only ill equipped, but unprepared for this war.

Modern combat boots were another thing the army was lacking. We had to make due with World War I canvas leggings. The leggings went over high top shoes to prevent sand and pebbles from getting in. A soldier can't walk very far with rocks in his shoes! Every time I went out in the rain on a march my shoes would leak like sieves. Regardless of how hard I tried to waterproof them, water always got in through the stitching where the soles were attached.

Wide waist belts were issued that were worn on the outside of our uniforms for holding canteens and bayonets. Pockets that attached to the belts were used for holding clips of ammunition.

Learning to work and march as a team was a job all its own. Day after day we would hike, each day a little longer and a little further. I had never walked long distances or carried this much equipment before, not to mention doing them simultaneously. After marching all day, I was about as exhausted as a human being could get. My feet throbbed and my skin felt grimy against my shirt from sweat and dust. Somehow I would recuperate the next day. I guess being young and in good shape made the difference.

Everybody dreaded getting blisters while marching. If this should happen, we were to immediately fall out and wait for the truck that picked up stragglers. The pain from blisters could incapacitate a soldier for days. The first stop would be the medic who lanced them and applied medicated ointment. I was lucky. I never got a blister. I used candle wax on the inside of the heels of my shoes as a precaution, a little something I learned in boy scout camp. Overseas, I used the wax I scraped off the outside of my K-rations.

This training was pushing me to my limits. It was certainly a real test of my endurance. Although my gut feeling told me that this was nothing compared to what I would face in the future. I was also pretty sure that once overseas, much more equipment would be added to my load. Training was the easy part, reality would be hell.

I never learned to use the different types of machine guns. At the beginning of the war, the army was using World War I water cooled, thirty caliber machine guns. The guns were accurate and effective, firing at the rate of more than five hundred rounds per minute. They were also big, heavy and hell to tote around. Modifications were made on the small machine guns to help cool and stabilize them by adding perforated metal covers and bipods to their barrels. Handles were added to the tops, making them easier to carry.

Gas mask classes were a treat. The Germans used several types of gases. Their effects were gruesome and almost always fatal. This provided a good incentive for practicing with my gas mask. Holding our masks in our hands we were led into a large tent filled with tear gas. The order was given to put the mask on. As fast as was humanly possible, I popped it on and made adjustments. Breathing tear gas is not a pleasant experience, to say the least. It wouldn't kill a man, but would make him violently ill and extremely disoriented. The instructor went from man to man pushing his fingers around the masks making sure they fit properly. We stayed in the tent about five minutes. It felt more like an eternity. As soon as we were dismissed, I scrambled out of that tent as fast as I could, tearing off my mask, and gasping for that wonderful, sweet smelling, fresh air.

The gas mask was designed for men who wore glasses. Spring loaded steel framed lenses could be installed in seconds when needed. In battle, a mask may

20

have had to be worn indefinitely. A soldier needed to see what he was doing and I was one of those soldiers who needed this feature. Luckily, I would never have need for my mask.

I had one lesson with the small mortar. Mortar ranges are large open fields. A mortar consists of three main parts: a steel tube about two feet high with an adjustable bipod attached to enable it to sit at an angle; a metal base plate that is placed on the ground that the tube sits on; and the mortar shells, which look like small rockets with fins on the bottom. Three men made up a mortar team. Each man was responsible for carrying different parts. Operating the mortar was quick and easy. One man stood on the left of it, another on the right, and one behind. The man behind held the shell, pulled the safety pin and handed the shell to the man on the right. The man on the right held the shell fins down at arm's length over the tube. He then dropped the shell into the tube, while simultaneously pulling his hand away from the tube. There was a loud thud and the shell was airborne. The man on the left acted as the spotter. He watched where the mortar hit and made sight adjustments. Once a mortar was set up it was possible for one man to operate.

I had a class on fragmentation hand grenades. A grenade range was a small area on a field that consisted of a waist high mound of sand with a pit on the other side of the mound. The grenade consisted of a cast iron main body, gun powder, a handle, a fuse and a cotter pin with a one inch diameter metal ring attached. This last part was the safety device. The grenade resembled a miniature pineapple. It was four and a half inches high, two and a half inches in diameter and weighed one pound. It was sized to fit perfectly in one's hand, hence the name. When a user pulls the safety pin, the grenade is immediately thrown at the planned target and the thrower ducks for cover. Within five seconds, the grenade explodes filling the air with hundreds of pieces of flesh shredding shrapnel, destroying anything within its radius. Everyone tossed a grenade into the pit to experience what it was like. It made a thunderous explosion that shook the ground and kicked up a cloud of smoke, sand and dust. It amazed me that something that small and simple was so extremely deadly. I gained a new respect for hand grenades. In combat, I usually carried them in my jacket pockets. When I carried them on my belt or strap, I always wrapped tape around the grenades, securing the handles for extra safety. I would not want one of these babies going off by accident!

After all my training and assigned courses were completed, I was allowed to go off base. They finally opened the cage and let me out! Aniston, Alabama was the nearest town and I was on my way. Once there, all I wanted to do was forget the day to day rigors of army life. I sat back with my buddies and had myself a great meal, a few cold beers and one hell of a good time. One thing was certain. From the moment I entered the army, I was constantly challenged to perform better than I ever had before. I was surprised by my own performance and exceeded my own expectations. I was now prepared physically, mentally and spiritually for whatever was in store for me. In retrospect, I feel I owe my life to the soldiers who trained me during those three intense months of basic training. It is my opinion that "they did the greatest job the world has ever seen!"

Days later, we said our good-byes and were split up into small groups and shipped out to camps all over the country. Sadly, I never again saw my compatriots from basic training, nor would I ever know if they survived this nightmare called war.

Rifle Range

Bayonet Training

Gas Mask Training

Hand to Hand Combat

27

.

Chapter 3
Transportation Corps

I was dispatched to a transportation corps in Newport News, Virginia. It was located twenty miles from Camp Patrick Henry and ten miles from the motor pool. This was a debarkation and disembarkation port that ran twenty four hours a day. I had no idea why I was sent here. But who was I to question the army in its infinite wisdom. I was assigned to the parts department in the motor pool division. Accommodations consisted of two story barracks right in town. This was fantastic! Who could ask for a better location? Nearby, where a park used to be, was a one story, half block long mess hall near an arch that looked like the Arc De Triomphe. Unlike some camps, there was only one mess hall and it was open twenty four hours a day. When the wind was in the right direction I could smell the delightful aromas all night long. Paid civilians worked on all the jobs. The up side was they did the latrine, cooking and cleaning duty.

The down side was they got a weekly salary while we got our army pay: fifty dollars per month. Because of this, there were hard feelings and no one would help the paid civilians.

I held a nine to five job, five or sometimes six days a week in the parts department. Alarm clocks woke us up unless someone had unusual hours, then an orderly woke him. Lights were left on all night in the doorways and latrines because of the twenty four hour day. Soldiers would come and go all hours. My morning routine was to wash, dress, make my bed and ready my room and my foot locker for inspection. On work days, after breakfast, I caught a military truck or bus that took men from the barracks to their various work stations. I came back for lunch and returned to work until quitting time and then went to dinner. After dinner I could go wherever I wanted. Already being in town, I stayed there until it got late and then headed over to the mess hall before going back to my barracks. Cold cuts and cheeses were laid out so everyone could make their own sandwiches. We could also have tea, coffee, hot chocolate or lemonade and a variety of cakes and pies. This was every night until eleven p.m. I felt like a kid in a candy store. On weekends, I would get a pass and visit relatives who lived not too far away in Norfolk, Virginia. They would always ask me to stay for dinner. All I could say was "this was living!"

The motor pool had been informed that the 45th Division was coming in with a massive job for us to do.

The motor pool could hold fifty vehicles in its bays for repairs and maintenance. Boy, was I going to be busy! Camp Patrick Henry was where the 45th Division would stay while the work was being done. The camp could easily hold a division, which was about fifteen thousand men, plus all their vehicles, cannons and equipment. While at the camp, the 45th would be issued fresh uniforms and equipment until their ship came. In all, this camp fielded twelve million men. Just think of the logistics of supplying them. It's mind boggling! While the 45th stayed here, they were not allowed into town. It was already over crowded from the army and naval personnel stationed nearby. Well, that just meant additional cold cuts for me.

The 45th was scheduled to go overseas. Before they left, their vehicles needed modifications that would render them water tight. Sparks of molten metal flew in every direction as men with welding equipment worked at a feverish rate, trying to meet deadlines. Curls of foul smelling smoke choked the air. The noise was so loud, I could hardly hear myself think. Tall pipes were added to the air intakes and exhausts, extending them above the vehicles. Now it was possible for the vehicles to travel through deep water or land on beaches without stalling. Hopefully, the electricity wouldn't short out.

I think I was stationed at Newport News for about nine months when we began getting called down to headquarters. All types of written tests, including I.Q., were being given. We weren't told what they were for, but knowing the army, something was up. A few days later our suspicions were confirmed. Anyone with high marks was being sent to some sort of advanced college course training program. It was called A.S.T.P. I can't recall what that stood for, but I was going. The commanding officer here didn't like the idea of losing men from his "kingdom", I mean camp. He issued orders not to release us. Well, we were not the only people who were unhappy about this decision. It appeared the commander stepped on a few toes. The army brass was furious. They weren't going to let him get away with this. They immediately issued new orders making it an official ruling. Anyone who passed the tests was going to A.S.T.P. I guess our commander lost this one because I was going.

Chapter 4
A. S. T. P.

Each of us were being sent to a college with a different type of specialty that matched our qualifications. The colleges were located all over the country but I was lucky. I didn't have far to travel. I was only going from the east coast of Virginia to the west side, to Virginia Polytechnic Institute in Blacksburg. I was taking engineering courses with one little twist. I had to carry twenty five credits in a three month semester. That was a heavy load to carry!

Military officers were in charge at the college. When we arrived, new clothing was issued. They gave us two pair of regular shoes instead of high tops, two sets of cotton suntan and two sets of olive wool uniforms. Suntan ties were worn with the olive shirts. Matching hats, overcoats and jackets completed the ensemble. This became quite a fashion show! The jackets were called blouses. The short version became known as an

Eisenhower Jacket, named after the esteemed General who made it popular. The older ones came with brass buttons, the newer with plastic, but we didn't have a choice. In order to dress up our coats we had tailors put in long pleats on each side of the back. Payment for the alteration was out of our own pockets, no pun intended. I was looking mighty snazzy in my new uniform.

Living accommodations were the regular college dorms. They were superb in comparison to army barracks. Identification pins, called "gig" pins, were worn on the front of our uniforms. Any time an officer saw someone doing something he wasn't supposed to he would look at his pin and write down his name on an infraction list. That's what we called getting "gigged". If a person received five infractions he was kicked out of the program. No one ever wanted that to happen. It meant being sent into an outfit that was going overseas.

Study, study, study! I was constantly studying. I had found my own private little office in which to study. Well, let me clarify that. Each dorm had a phone booth in the lobby and I sort of took it over whenever I could. But like all good things, it came to an end when the school replaced the bulb with a smaller one that didn't provide enough light to read.

I was doing okay in the army. Over one year had passed and I still had not seen combat. No complaints there. I had already completed two semesters. That was fifty credits I had under my belt. About one hundred fifteen were needed to graduate with a four year degree.

Unfortunately, I would never get the chance to finish. Just as fast as the army could start a program, it could disband one, and so the college program came to an abrupt halt. All the soldiers in every college were being shipped out to different divisions. Now I had something new to worry about. Where was the army sending me?

Looking Good for School

Chapter 5
84th Infantry Division

I ended up in the 84th Infantry Division, Camp Claiborne, Louisiana which was called the Lincoln Division, or "The Rail Splitter Division". At the time of my transfer, the division was on spring maneuvers in some Godforsaken swamp in the middle of Louisiana. Here I was stomping around through a swamp, dressed for college, wearing a shirt and tie, a jacket and low shoes. I don't know which was worse, the oppressive heat, humidity or stench. I was a dripping mess, still carrying my books: perfect! The only thing I could be thankful for was that maneuvers were finished in a week. Then at least, I could be properly outfitted. I wasn't alone in my predicament. A guy with whom I later became buddies was sent here from the University of Pennsylvania.

Rumor had it that this division was in poor shape. The army had sent a group of fresh college men in to help turn things around. It was thought a better division could be made by adding more brain power; only time would tell.

Many of the men here were Indians from Florida and Louisiana. One thing I remember about them was they loved hot sauce. A little bottle of red sauce was placed on every table in the mess hall. They splashed this stuff in and on everything they ate. It didn't matter what it was as long as it had plenty of hot sauce on it. They even spent some of their allotted company funds on hot sauce. God bless them, they must have had iron clad stomachs.

Just when I started getting comfortable here the army came along and screwed things up. There was a surplus of men. The remedy was to take every fifth new transferee and send him to another outfit, regardless of whether he were needed there or not. Needless to say, I was a fifth name on the list.

Chapter 6
555th Signal Corps

I was packing and taking a little trip to Texas, Fort Sam Houston, that is. This was the home of the 555th Signal Corps repair depot. The men here were fully trained repairmen, schooled in electronic repair for field telephones, radios, etc. The group of us sent here didn't know anything about repair: another army S.N.A.F.U.? One consolation was we would live in beautiful two story brick barracks with finished floors. A dilemma arose: what to do with us? Given enough time I knew the army would find something for us to do, and they did! They found a solution to two problems. This battalion was due to go overseas. Before the men could leave they had to pass different qualification tests. Since we were in pretty good shape it became our job to ready the men for their tests. They had to pass rifle range testing even though as repairmen they may never have had to use a rifle. We put them through their paces on twenty five mile endurance hikes. These guys weren't used to this kind of training. They were in sorry shape. There was this one day when we were out on a march and I had started out all the way in the rear of the column. So many men had slowed their pace or dropped out from exhaustion, that by the end of the march I was way ahead of the front of the column.

Just like the other places I had been, there was a problem of too many new men. Gee, what a surprise! The army had to split us up and ship us out to different outfits again. While waiting to leave, we heard that the Paratroop Division was looking for volunteers. This big, tall fellow with large meaty hands and dark bushy eyebrows that met in the middle named Daly said, "Come on Jack let's go down and try out". I remember his name because we always had a problem when roster was called. Danish and Daly sounded similar when bellowed out. Daly eventually convinced a bunch of us to go and try out. What did we have to lose? I wore glasses. Because of this I was unable to qualify. In fact, I'd always carried extra glasses in a metal case in my right rear pocket. Overseas I would also carry an extra pair in my gas mask case. Some of the men passed all the qualifying tests and were transferred over. The rest of us hung around day after day waiting to be shipped out. What made it worse was that nobody could tell us when we were leaving or where we were going. The army found something to occupy our time while waiting. They put us to work at the supply office. Now we spent our days stacking uniforms and assorted other goods. This was boredom at its best. The consensus was we were all fed up with being shipped from outfit to outfit, then doing and accomplishing nothing.

Eventually orders came though and some of us were dispatched to Camp Bowie, to the 1299th Combat Engineer Battalion near the town of Brownwood, Texas. Here I go again... pack up, move out!

Paratroop Tryouts

Paratroop Tryouts

Chapter 7
1299th Engineer Batalion

There I was again, changing all the insignias on my uniforms and hats. The Army Corps of Engineers' insignia was the castle.

Having been a private for a long time I was hoping to acquire a promotion. Some of the men shipped here had resigned their rank just to get into the A.S.T.P. program. They were hoping for advancement also.

This Engineer Battalion was made up of four companies. Companies A, B, & C, were the line companies and in charge of the bridge building and the equipment needed. Company H & S or Headquarters and Services, my company, was responsible for the collection and purification of water and the equipment used to accomplish the tasks. I was being trained to be a water supply technician. A good percentage of our time was spent practicing the speed with which we could ready the equipment for use. We drove our water supply truck to a nearby stream where we proceeded to set up a three thousand gallon heavy gauge collapsible canvas water tank. The tank stood shoulder high and about twelve foot across. Carved hardwood support staves were pushed into vertical sleeves on the sides of the tank. Ropes were used to stake down the tank. Four ropes were wrapped around the tank to adjust it. A portable gasoline driven water pump with two fire hoses attached was used to fill the tank. One hose went into the stream with a filtering screen on the end to protect the pump from rock damage. The other hose was put over the top of the tank. Water was pumped through a one hundred pound sand filter and chlorinating chemicals were added for purification. Test kits were used to check for pH balance, poisons and bacterium. Upon completion of the tank filling, we drove for miles putting up painted signs along the roadsides saying "water" with an arrow pointing the direction. Our location was also noted on the area maps. Not long after staking the signs, all different types of trucks started arriving. Some were big one thousand gallon tanker trucks, others were filled with dozens of five gallon gerry cans. Filling trucks with water would go on for hours.

I was learning the art of building bridges. All four companies took part. Bridges came in numerous sizes, shapes and types. There were narrow foot bridges, gigantic floating bridges and wooden trestle bridges. Some looked like immense erector sets. The floating bridges were assembled to cross water. The base of the floating bridges consisted of rectangular, flat bottomed, wooden barges. Wooden trestles were constructed over ravines. It took twenty stout men to carried the long-spliced timbers to the bridge site. Eight to ten sections were connected and laid on metal plates and rollers. Men built up the approach with the help of dynamite blasting and then refilled the area with stones. The bridge began to take shape. The front was faced upward to compensate for sagging as we pushed the sections across the chasm with the help of trucks. The process was repeated until the bridge was completed. This was grueling work. Engineers were taught to go under, over or through anything, or get it out of the way. Our ultimate mission was to keep the army moving, moving towards victory.

My day started every morning at five thirty. The bugle playing reveille was my alarm clock. I was already accustomed to rising early even before I joined the army. I had fifteen minutes to get out and line up for roll call. Everyone rushed to the latrine, washed their faces and got dressed. There was one guy in our barracks who made a daily routine of getting in an extra ten minutes of sleep. To do this he waited until the last second, jumped out of bed in his underwear, pulled on his boots and threw on his hat and overcoat. He scurried outside and got in the lineup, just in time for roll call. It just didn't seem worth it to me. At roll call an officer would bellow out each man's last name. Each man responded by shouting "here!" When all were present or accounted for we were dismissed. Some of us would go back to the barracks, wash up and dress for breakfast. Others would line up at the mess hall and wait for the breakfast call which was exactly fifteen minutes after roll call. The bugler played a song called "Come and Get Your Beans Boys". That signaled the mess hall was open. The army had a motto in the mess hall. "Take all you want but eat all you take." After breakfast we lined up on the parade grounds for the raising of the flag. Then it was back to the barracks to prepare for daily inspection. One hour was allotted to accomplish the task. Every minute was needed to clean the floors, windows, foot lockers and make our beds with hospital corners. Keeping the raw wood floors clean was a full time job. Dirt was constantly accumulating in the cracks of the wood and was hard as hell to get out. If there were any time left over we could get in a quick shave and shower. When someone didn't pass inspection their name went on an infraction list that was posted on our bulletin board along with what was wrong. Whatever was wrong needed to be corrected immediately. After inspection we reported to our assigned jobs and worked until eleven thirty. Then, it was back to the barracks to wash up before lunch. The bugle blared at twelve sharp for lunch. After finishing lunch we could go back to the barracks to do whatever we wanted until one p.m., then it was back to work. Four thirty was quitting time and back to the barracks to clean up and dress up for retreat, the lowering of the flag. We assembled on the parade grounds for the ceremony. The bugle would play as the flag was lowered. Six o'clock was dinner time and the bugle sounded again. After dinner we were free to do whatever we wanted as long as we stayed on base. Some of us went back to the barracks to write letters to loved ones. Others went to the P.X. (post exchange) to buy things like beer, soda, cards and candy, or just to relax and socialize with other soldiers. The P.X. stayed open every night until nine. At this post, movies were shown almost every night. At ten the bugler played taps. The song was "Day is Done". This also meant "lights out" and no noise in the barracks. There was no set time we had to be in the barracks to go to sleep. As long as we showed up for roll call the next day everyone was happy. Sometimes a few of us sat outside the barracks and chatted until early in the morning. With a pass, we could stay in town all night.

Saturday morning was always the big inspection. If we had no assignment and were lucky enough to get a class "A" pass, the weekend was all ours. But if we had guard duty it was a whole different story.

Guard duty was one of those dreaded dirty words right up there with "kitchen police" (the infamous "K.P.") and "latrine duty". It was one pain in the ass twenty four hour assigned tour. Sometimes it was two hours on and two hours off. Other times it was four hours on and four hours off. I preferred the four hour shift. It allowed me to get a little sleep. I was unable to sleep on the two hour shift. Normal routines didn't apply when assigned to guard duty. Arrangements were made ahead of time with the roll call and mess hall officers. At the mess hall, the cooks always took special care of us. Our eating was done either before or after normal meal time. Even late at night, the cooks saw to it that we were fed. On one of my assignments, I walked back and forth between trucks in the motor pool. I had to carry my rifle at all times, despite the fact I was not permitted to load it. The reasoning behind this brilliant idea was so officers wouldn't mistakenly get shot when periodically sneaking up to check if we were sitting or sleeping. As a guard I felt useless. There were never any incidents of trucks being stolen or sabotaged. This was nothing but a waste of time and energy. If there were a problem, all I could do was call out for the corporal of the guard. The only time I ever found him useful was when I couldn't wait until my break to use the toilet. He was the one who would either get someone to relieve my post or do it himself. The maximum I would ever need was only ten minutes. Late at night I wouldn't even bother calling for relief. I would just urinate between the trucks. I figured no one would ever know and after twenty four hours I was too exhausted to care.

To my dismay, I had heard that the army was shipping in a considerable amount of men from all the antiaircraft outfits that were set up all over the country. The army originally thought we would be attacked by airplanes from ships offshore. This never came to pass so these outfits were being disbanded. The men from these outfits all held high ranks. There were two stripe and three stripe sergeants and so on. An outfit normally had one top sergeant. We would now have four. There went any chance of my ever being promoted in rank here! Having no rank had serious disadvantages. It meant always getting stuck doing all the menial jobs. A whole group of us in this situation got stuck doing latrine duty. Who the hell wants to clean toilets all day? Then, there was K.P. duty. That's another job we all loathed. We worked like slaves in the mess hall. Our day started at five in the morning and if we were lucky we finished at ten in the evening. There were no breaks during the day except to eat. We were responsible for doing everything except cooking. The army had cooks for that job. Food was served cafeteria style and we did the serving. There were five separate tables reserved for officers. We had to serve these prima donnas at their tables. They acted as if they were in a damn restaurant. Those sons of bitches even left their dishes on the tables after eating. This was just plain laziness and an abuse of their rank. Everyone else in the mess hall had to take their own dishes off the table. It aggravated us that the post commander was allowing this type of behavior. It also made that much more extra work for us. We were in charge of cleaning everything, including scrubbing every inch of the interior of this place. You name it, we cleaned it! On top of that, we had one mess hall sergeant who loved boiling bars of soap and pouring the mixture all over the floors. He would start doing this at seven p.m. We were trying to get finished so we could leave. It took hours to mop that mess up. It was not that he was a rotten guy. He just had this idiosyncrasy about how to clean the floors. He worked long hard hours along side of us, but didn't care how long it took to clean the floors this way. He could sleep late the next day. He worked a one day on one day off shift. We had to get up the next morning bright and early for training or work.

After months of cleaning the floors in this fashion, soapy water started leaking through and getting under the building, rotting the beams. The post commander finally put a stop to this cleaning practice. He had no idea how happy he made us.

With all the new people pouring into our outfit there was a surplus. A call for men came in from the 1285th Combat Engineer Battalion. The 1299th and the 1285th shared the same camp. The 1285th was going overseas in the near future and needed to fill their ranks. Seven men and I were transferred over to the 1285th. I wasn't sorry to leave the 1299th after all the rotten jobs I had been given. Well, it looked like I was going to see Europe after all. It just wasn't the way I would have chosen to go.

Retreat: *I'm in front row at the end.*

Chapter 8
1285th Engineer Battalion

Before a battalion could go overseas, all the men had to pass a series of different qualification tests. This was almost like starting all over again.

Many new pieces of equipment were being issued. A novel type of knapsack that had compartments was quite an improvement over the World War I knapsacks. Unpacking dozens of things in order to use my blanket was no longer necessary. The blanket sat on the top along with a tent half. Every soldier carried a half of a tent. Halves buttoned together completing one tent for two soldiers. In inclement weather, three soldiers used one tent. The extra half was used as a ground sheet to help keep us dry. We had heard that once overseas, we would receive a modern sleeping bag that could be used on the ground or placed on a cot. Having never seen a sleeping bag before, I wasn't certain what it was going to look like.

The army gave us real combat boots: no more leaky shoes! I had always kept my boy scout knife with me as a good luck charm. From this point on I carried it in my right boot. We received the latest design in helmets. These helmets had a chin strap with a ball and socket joint that would pop apart allowing the helmet to come off without injuring the man. Pressure from an explosion can tear a helmet off a soldier's head breaking his jaw or worse.

New belts that held our canteens, bayonets, ammunition and grenades were issued. There were eight small pockets on the belts, each one big enough to hold an ammunition clip. Three quarter inch wide cotton bandoleers with five covered pockets attached was for carrying extra ammo. These would be given to us overseas. The army was weighing us down with equipment as if we were human pack horses. After giving it more thought, whatever I could carry, I would. I didn't want to run out of anything while in battle. Every piece of equipment would be necessary for survival.

Spanking new, modern, U.S. made semiautomatic M1 Garand rifles were issued. This baby weighed approximately ten pounds and had an eight bullet clip. This was some rifle! There was nothing like it in the world. I was impressed. I was being well equipped compared to soldiers of other countries that would fight this war. Quick courses were given to familiarize us with our new weapon. During house to house combat training my rifle kept sticking and jamming. I just could not get it to fire properly. I hoped this wasn't an omen. Right then and there, I took that sucker apart on the hood of a truck. I couldn't see what was malfunctioning. Crossing my fingers, I squirted some oil on the parts and reassembled it. I never again had a problem with my rifle, thank God!

Combat Engineer Battalions never used mortars. We relied on rifle grenades as replacements. Rifle grenades were reasonably accurate. Each man was equiped with eight grenades and the eight blank cartridges necessary for firing them. Blanks had a red plug on the end to distinguish them from live ammunition. Using the standard bullet would cause the grenade to explode, killing its user. To be safe, I always kept my blanks in a separate pocket. The launching device for the grenade slipped over the rifle's muzzle. A grenade was pushed onto the device just before firing. Launches could at least triple the distance we could throw hand grenades. With a little luck, I would be able to blow the tread off an enemy tank.

Bangalore tubes were carried overseas for blowing pathways through barbed wire. It was nothing but a very long, capped pipe loaded with an explosive with a primer cap and fuse that was lit by hand. When we couldn't go around the barbed wire we slid the tube under and blew it apart. Barbed wire was set up in triangular shapes using hundreds of strands. Usually, mines were placed around the perimeter. This made doing the job even more treacherous.

I was never given the course on flame throwers. The idea of being in combat with two large tanks filled with jellied gasoline on my back just didn't sit well with me. I had to learn how to make jellied gasoline. It turned out to be a very simple process. I took an empty fifty five gallon drum, filled it with gasoline and added one packet of special powder into the gasoline. Using a water tank stave I stirred the mixture. It was easy: just mix and serve.

Overseas, every tenth man in my battalion would carry a bazooka. It was mainly used against tanks and armor-plated personnel carriers, but only when in close proximity to its intended target. A bazooka rocket that hit its mark would leave a gaping hole and make one hell of a thunderous explosion. I was not required to take this course, although having seen one used, I could hook it up and fire it.

Combat Engineers had the dangerous and tricky job of removing the many types of mines and booby traps the Germans loved using. In this job, your first mistake was your last. It took an enormous amount of patience, nerve and prayer. To help find mined areas, we used mine detectors. From that point on, every inch of ground was checked while crawling on our bellies. We probed the ground with our bayonets until we hit metal or wires. Once we disarmed a mine, we moved on looking for the next, leaving a trail of white tape behind us so soldiers knew where it was safe to walk. This was another class in which everyone gave their undivided attention.

There was a short class given on first aid. Overseas we would all carried small first aid kits that attached to our belts. They contained a bandage and sulpha pills. The pills were some sort of antibiotic. If wounded we were to use the kit until a medic could get to us. The army also gave us pills to put in our drinking water. Being a water supply technician, I didn't need the pills.

The 1285th needed more fifty caliber machine gunners. I was sent into the desert for a fourteen day, non-stop, crash course at Camp Santa Anna, New Mexico, just outside El Paso, Texas. The heat was insufferable! There was also no time off, not even on Sunday. There was no chaplain, no services, not even a P.X. It was strictly business.

Unlike rifle ranges, machine gun ranges are huge designated open areas that bombers, DC3's and drones flew over towing target sleeves. The drones themselves became targets. Fifty caliber machine guns were used against aircraft but were just as effective for ground fire. The body of the gun was two foot long, weighed fifty pounds, had a thirty inch long barrel weighing twenty pounds. It fired a bullet one half of an inch in diameter and one inch long, with a shell casing that was four inches long. No small potatoes! This gun devoured tremendous amounts of ammunition within seconds. It produced a deafening repetitious roar, while filling the air with brief streaks of ruddy light, like some fire spitting monster. Ammunition was fed into the side of the gun on a belt. A small machine was used to attach several types of bullets to the feed belt. The sequence was three regular rounds, one armor piercing round and one tracer round to assist in aiming the machine gun. Preparation of the belts was performed while waiting our turn to fire the gun. This also kept our thoughts off the sauna like conditions.

At the range, guns were mounted on chest high poles. There were two guide poles a few yards in front of, on either side of the mounting pole, forming a triangle. Firing the gun was done by a team of three men. One fired the gun. One stood on the side of the gun feeding in the ammunition. The last stood behind the shooter to help spot the target and aim the gun. An airplane flew by towing a target. When the target reached the parameter of a side pole, the spotter tapped the shooter's helmet to cue him to fire. The shooter held the gun by handles, one on each side, and pressed a butterfly shaped trigger in the center with his thumbs. The shooter fired following the target, trying not to hit the tow plane. Because of the loud noise the gun produced, the spotter had to rap hard on the shooter's helmet to cue him to cease fire once the target reached the other parameter. The total sweep of firing was around one hundred twenty degrees. We each took turns performing the different jobs, but agreed that firing the gun was the most fun.

Fifty caliber machine guns were used on jeeps, six by six trucks and on the ground. When used on jeeps, they were mounted on tall poles. When used on trucks, they were mounted on huge rings on the cabs' roofs.

Holes had been cut in the roofs on the passenger sides so the shooter could stand on the seat, his body sticking through the roof in the center of the ring. The gun could be swung around on the ring in every direction.

A tripod was mounted on the gun for ground use. It took a team of men to carry all the parts, which included three extra barrels. Firing the gun for any length of time would heat the barrel, causing it to warp slightly and lose accuracy. Periodically, the barrel needed to be changed during a skirmish. This was a harrowing experience. Barrels got so hot that asbestos gloves needed to be used to unscrew them from the guns. Hot barrels were placed on the ground to cool, then they would be reused. When the guns were mounted on trucks, the hot barrels were tossed into one half of a fifty five gallon drum filled with water that was affixed to the trucks. Boy, when that barrel hit the water, would it hiss, sizzle and spew steam!

After fourteen grueling days of extreme heat, profuse sweating and intensive training, we headed back to Camp Bowie, Texas to link up with the rest of the 1285th.

I was now a Combat Engineer with three specialties: rifleman, water supply technician and fifty caliber machine gunner. I was sure my specialties would be put to use very soon.

Chapter 9
Going Overseas

About a month later, the 1285th Engineer Battalion was packing in preparation to go overseas. Orders had come down from headquarters to be prepared to move on a moment's notice. Days later, we were on our way. Trucks brought us to a railroad station where we boarded trains headed for New Jersey. We remained at Camp Shanks, New Jersey, for about one week. Every afternoon passes were issued and everyone headed across the Hudson River to Manhattan. Many of the men were from small towns and anxious to see this famous big city. Unfortunately, this might be their last chance to ever see an American city again. I spent the time visiting my family and fiancee. It was great being home again, even if it were only for a short time. Hey, you just can't beat those home cooked meals. I was asked the usual questions about military life, like how was the army treating me and was I getting enough to eat. Time flew by rapidly. It hardly felt like a week had passed and there I was saying my good-byes. I received enough hugs, kisses and tears to last me until I returned home again.

It was Thanksgiving, 1944. The weather was mild and the trees were shedding the last of their leaves. My battalion was getting ready to leave Camp Shanks. The rest of the camp was getting ready to sit down to the army's best meal of the year, a turkey dinner, when it dawned on the officers that they hadn't made provisions to feed us. This was a S.N.A.F.U. of titanic proportions as far as we were concerned. The only thing they were able to scrounge up was peanut butter and jelly sandwiches and coffee. Seating arrangements were terrible. We had to sit where we stood and eat. What a Thanksgiving sendoff this was!

An hour later we lined up on the New Jersey docks waiting for special ferries to take us across the Hudson River to pier 88, New York. There we would board troop ships. Our destination was Southampton, England.

Everywhere I looked, there were thousands of men pouring in from every direction. On the dock, near the ship I was to board, the Red Cross was giving out donuts and coffee. I was never one to pass up coffee and donuts. I quickly ran over and grabbed some. I took a long sip from the paper cup and bit into the donut. It might be the last taste of civilization for a long time, although I would have preferred apple pie for the occasion. The ship I boarded was a converted Caribbean cruise liner once named the U.S.S. California. It was now a troop transporter. The open decks had been sealed in with huge sheets of steel and every available space was being utilized. The smell of fresh paint lingered on every deck. Sleeping bunks were stacked four high. My clothing had been crammed into a big green duffel bag with a shoulder strap attached. I hated that damn bag! If I needed one thing and it happened to be on the bottom, the whole damn bag had to be unpacked. Speaking about being packed, if they had put one more man on this ship, it would have sunk. Now I know what sardines feel like. Each outfit was confined to an assigned section on the ship. Whenever it was time to eat, smoke or exercise we had to wait until our section's name was announced over the loudspeaker. The optimum word here was wait! When it was chow time we got on a line that snaked through the ship until we reached the mess hall or galley. The food was picked up cafeteria style. There was no room to sit. Tables were chest high with lips on the edge so as the ship listed things wouldn't slide off. We stood wherever there was an opening. The next line was for the toilet or head. Some days this wait could be a real challenge. It's not easy to walk with one's legs crossed. We waited to exercise. It was nothing more than getting to an outside deck and stretching, although breathing fresh air was a nice change. This was how I spent the better part of my day.

The ship headed north toward Boston. About two hundred miles off the coast, our ship rendezvoused with a convoy of a few hundred ships. We looked in astonishment. As far as we could see, in every direction, there were ships of every description. If I were a giant, I could walk across the ocean by stepping on them. At the head of the convoy was a massive British battleship. Troopships remained in the center of the convoy. Surrounding the troopships were dozens of destroyers, cruisers, corvettes, tankers, mine sweepers and cargo ships. It certainly gave me a sense of security.

It took almost two weeks to get to England, but at least we made it. I was glad to have my feet on solid ground again. I had enough rocking back and forth to last me a lifetime. At least I hadn't gotten seasick like so many of the other men.

Chapter 10
England

Our landing in Southampton was at night. It was so dark, I could barely see anything as I boarded a train at the pier. I had no idea what direction the train was traveling or where I was headed. After a considerably long and bumpy ride, the train arrived at its destination. Now it was time for all of us to stretch our legs and march the rest of the way to wherever we were going. An hour later our journey ended at an old towering castle in the countryside called the Addle Strop Estate, in a town called Stowe on the Wold. The castle was owned by a Lord Leigh, whoever he was? The castle became our headquarters. A quonset hut village built into the hillside would be my new living quarters. Quonset huts are pre-fabricated portable huts having semicircular roofs of cor-rugated metal that curve down to form walls. They look like big tin cans that have been laid on their sides. Each one held twenty five to thirty men. It was winter so we had to keep the coal stove in the middle of the place burning. The trouble was there was no coal here. There was only coke, which looks like burnt out coal or lava rock and didn't give much heat. To add to this, the huts dissipated heat rapidly. Straw was given to us to stuff mattress covers we would use to sleep on. Luckily, we had real pillows and blankets. I felt like I was in a barn. Even a prisoner would have complained about these living conditions. I spent a month or so here and found the weather to always be any combination of four miserable things: nasty, wet, foggy or cold! The countryside was quite hilly and muddy. The castle was down hill from where we stayed. This is where headquarters was set up and where we ate. Before heading back into the murk and mud to our huts, we always picked up coke for the stove. No one ever wanted to make an extra trip if they didn't have to.

Our days were consumed with fine tuning our training along side the 1133rd Combat Engineer Group, who was also stationed here. The training was done by the 69th Infantry Division in a place called Upton Lovel. My battalion became so proficient at building Bailey bridges, that we had been chosen for the Rhine River crossing. I spent many days honing my skills at the rifle range at a place called Wallingford, along with marching through the countryside to stay in shape.

Lectures were given on what to do if taken prisoner. The army's position was, "give only your name, rank and serial number!" We heard the German army didn't treat their prisoners very well, to say the least. In Europe, I would be traveling in a small group far from my headquarters for long periods of time, never knowing where I was going next. There would be times when I had no idea what country I was in! I'd be lucky if I knew what month or day it was, let alone important military information. I knew absolutely zilch! If taken prisoner and interrogated, I'd tell them anything they wanted to hear, even if I had to invent it all. Why should I take a beating or get killed for not cooperating? I wanted to survive this war! There were many men in my company who felt the same way. The two things I worried about most were: being captured or getting wounded and freezing to death. No one wants to suffer a slow, agonizing death. If it was going to happen, I wanted it to be fast and painless.

It was time again to pack up, load our equipment on the trucks and head for the other coast of England, to a place called Weymouth. This was the nearest debarkation point to France and that's where I was headed next. In Weymouth, gigantic underground, steel reinforced concrete bunkers had been built. The ceilings were at least three feet thick. If the facility were bombed, the men inside would be protected, and damage would be minimal. Equipment could always be replaced, lives couldn't. The mess hall was immense and able to serve thousands of men at a time. Surprisingly the food tasted pretty good. We only stayed over one night. The next day we headed for LeHarvre, France: enemy territory. This was what I had spent those months preparing for.

Anyone who wasn't a little scared now was either a fool or a liar.

Chapter 11
France

We removed the camouflage nets from our trucks and set out under the cover of darkness, making our way towards the docks. L.S.T.'s (landing ship tanks) and L.C.I.'s (landing craft infantries) were waiting to take us across the English Channel. The L.S.T. transported dozens of trucks, tanks and men. An L.C.I. only carried men. Small car-like boats called D.U.K.S. were also used. They had wheels like cars but could only drive off beaches. I can't recall what D.U.K.S. stood for but they only held about twelve men. Other ships were there to escort us across the Channel. German submarines may be lying in wait ready to sink any ship that tried to cross. We heard there had been a submarine attack the day before we arrived. A ship was sunk, there were no survivors. I don't know about anyone else but I had a bad feeling about this.

Part way across the channel the unthinkable happened. We were under attack! I could hear a Canadian Corvette sounding the alarm. Whoop! Whoop! Whoop! This sound was immediately followed by ear shattering booms of depth charges that echoed everywhere. Being in an L.S.T. was like being in a big tin can. It magnified the sound and vibrated violently. It was dark so I could only hear what was going on. The seamen on the boat were running to their battle stations yelling, "get out of the way!" They were scrambling to man small automatic cannons on the sides of the boat. Men's faces turned sheet white. I felt helpless but couldn't just stand there. Gritting my teeth, I leaped up onto one of the trucks and uncovered the fifty caliber machine gun. Clipping in an ammo belt and pulling back the bolt, I was ready to get my licks in if the sub should surface. I wiped the sweat from my face and waited as the seconds ticked off. I stood there with a cold misty wind blowing in my face. I only heard the hollow, slapping sound of the water. It made my flesh crawl. I sat down as my trembling legs gave way. I took a deep breath and exhaled slowly. It had ended just as it had started, with an eerie feeling. I realized I wasn't just a kid anymore. I had reacted as I was trained to, as a soldier.

I never did find out what had happened, but who cared. I survived and that's all that really mattered.

Battleships had already spent two days pummeling the main beaches with sixteen inch artillery shells. When we landed, there was no opposition. The heavy bombardment had cleared the beaches and left a maze of enormous craters. The battleships were softening up the enemy inland. Artillery shells flew overhead, screaming through the air. The sound alone was enough to scare anyone. I couldn't even imagine what the bigger shells must have sounded like. The City of Le Havre was a port and the army needed it for the millions of tons of supplies that would follow, so the port facilities were left intact. I was in the second wave to hit the beach. The gaping mouth of the landing craft opened. Soldiers were rushing us off screaming, "keep moving!" Groups of men were getting off in vehicles. The L.S.T. I was on got stuck on a sandbar. I jumped off into four feet of lapping water and kept moving forward, never looking back. I was soaked to the skin and would be walking around for days like this until everything dried out. What a way to start a day!

Mass confusion is the only way I could describe the scene on the beach. Men and equipment were everywhere. Trucks were getting bogged down in the sand. We were sitting ducks! It was imperative to get off this beach in a hurry in case of a counter attack. Luckily, my outfit, H & S Company, had been on the same L.S.T., which made it easier to stick together in all the confusion. We moved inland, regrouped and reorganized all our equipment. Without our equipment we were worthless, nothing but a bunch of soldiers standing around with rifles. A decision was made to move us a few miles inland just past Le Havre to a camp called "Twenty Grand".

Overnight camps, named after different cigarette brands, had been set up all through France, this being one of them. It was a place to stay a day, to eat and rest. It was too hard, slow and dangerous to take the vehicles through the fields, so we stuck to the main roads to get there. If the Germans ever caught us in an open field they would chew us up with their artillery. The Germans were effecient when it came to war, and they were extremely well equipped. The rutted road we were traveling on went straight for a long distance, then curved like a snake through the countryside. There was sporadic resistance and sniper fire, but for the most part, the Germans had evacuated the immediate area.

At the camp I was finally able to relax and let my guard down. It's not easy being on full alert every second. To say I had been scared would be an understatement. I was worn out! My skin was gritty from the salt water and dust from the road. I could not wait to wash up and sack out. I was glad this part of our journey was over. Later that day, I settled in, cradled my rifle and watched rays of light flicker between the trees as the sun went down. The foul odor of a cigar hung in the air. It made my throat raw. I took a swallow of warm, metallic tasting water from my canteen. Some leaked between my lips spilling on my coat. I just shrugged and wiped it off. I began wondering how I would feel the first time I engaged the enemy face to face? Could I pull the trigger without hesitation? It's easy shooting at paper targets, but this time I would be taking human lives. I would hear them scream out in agony, see them pitch and fall, smell the stench of blood and burnt gunpowder, as the life would drain from their bodies; this all taking place in the time it takes to draw a breath. What kind of insanity is this? Will it ever end? Then reality hit me! I am a soldier, and have a job to do. I know in my heart there's nothing pleasant about killing, even if it is to win a war. Besides, if I don't fire first, that will be me on the ground. Mentally exhausted, I pulled my helmet over my eyes and fell into an uneasy sleep.

Chapter 12
First Engagement

It was a clear, cool morning as we headed for the City of Caen. The British needed help in capturing the city. The German army never gave up easily. The British had already suffered heavy casualties on this one lousy city, that could have been surrounded and by-passed, until the Germans surrendered. Our army had done this very thing in the City of Brest on the coast of France. The Germans refused to give up. It was too costly in lives to storm the city, so we encircled the Germans and left a minimal amount of troops to keep them there, cutting off their supplies. We nicknamed these troops the "Brassiere Boys" because they were holding Brest. Months later the Germans surrendered with no loss of life on either side.

We joined up with the Brits and swung into action, launching our attack with the poise, precision and audacity of a seasoned outfit. The Germans were dug in and had ample time to fortify their positions. All that was visible were flashes from their weapons. Mesmerized by the sights, I forgot about the danger to myself as I pushed forward. Hearing bullets whizzing by my ear jolted me back to reality. My heart started pounding like that of a racehorse at full gallop. I was freezing, yet soaked with sweat. The land echoed with the thunder of battle. German mortar shells we nicknamed "screaming meemies" screeched and screamed like some mad woman, as they catapulted toward us. The ear piercing sound shook me to the core. The exploding shells shattered trees, sending hot shards of wood and flesh-shredding shrapnel in every direction. The shock waves tore the leaves from surrounding trees sending them swirling through the air. A burst of machine gun fire rang out. I dove for cover as bullets raked the ground around me, kicking up earth and debris. Men fell, their bodies a patchwork of scarlet. Wounded soldiers screamed in agony. An acrid smell filled the air. Men were shouting for medics. My stomach knotted as I gasped for air. I gagged and swallowed hard. It left a sour taste in my mouth. Everything was happening so fast. There was never time to think, only react. I pressed on through the barrage, fighting with a vengeance. Smoke flowed from the barrel of my rifle as it bucked against my shoulder. I was running across a field of dead soldiers, their bodies covering the land like scattered sticks of wood. The enemy troops held their ground like obstinate mules. The intensity of the battle seemed to impel men to extend themselves beyond expectations. In the face of withering enemy fire, we began making headway, but it was painfully slow and bloody. The turning point came when we finally rammed our way through the center of the city. Shooting slowed to sporadic gunfire. The siege was over. Only the menace of sniper fire and booby traps needed to be eliminated. What seemed like only minutes had actually been hours. It was a hard fought, costly battle, but our unrelenting combined force offensive had overwhelmed and decimated the Germans. I had performed my job like a soldier who had been doing this all his life. I felt proud of having survived my first engagement, yet shaken by all I had seen. The experience of this first battle was enough to last me a lifetime.

It was time to regroup, check on wounded friends and roundup prisoners. The air smelled rank. Shattered streets and buildings stood in silent testimony to the fierce pounding the city had received. Broken, bleeding German corpses littered the ground. Some lay frozen in time, still clutching their rifles. Others lay badly twisted with ghastly wounds, crying in agony, twitching, waiting to die. Overwhelmed and exhausted, things seemed to be closing in on me. I had a shaky, hollow feeling, like I was being sucked into some black abyss. I wiped the perspiration from my face and shook my head to clear it. I saw dazed looks and vacant expressions in the eyes and faces of friends. We were all part of the "living dead". I wanted to run and get away from this carnage filled hell hole, but duty wouldn't allow. I had to look away a minute or I'd be sick again.

Disarming many of the prisoners was unnecessary. They stood, hands raised high or behind their heads. They had already thrown their rifles, guns and knives on the ground. By surrendering, their chances of getting home were good. Home: there's a place I'd like to be right now! Weapons were collected and put into piles. I couldn't believe the amount of armament they had. The German army was exceptionally well equipped. If a prisoner were caught with a weapon, he would be shot where he stood, no questions asked. Prisoners had to be marched to the rear to Headquarters for interrogation. Not many men could be spared for this job. I marched about fifty prisoners with the help of only one other soldier. I marched at the rear holding a submachine gun while the other man marched at the front of the group. A translator told the prisoners that I was a Jew. They glanced at me with fear in their eyes. I grinned and pulled my index finger across my throat in a fast slashing motion. Now they were scared that I was going to kill them just because they were Germans. I yelled "march" in German and off we went. No one ever stepped out of line or gave me any trouble from that point on. If they did, they would be dead.

No one ever discussed the battles afterward or spoke about how they felt. We just took a breather from reality and stared into the distance. No one needed to say a word, we all understood. I never questioned being say a word, we all understood. I never questioned being alive after a battle. I was just glad that I was.

Now we sat here waiting for the army to pull us out of here so we could wash, rest and get some decent food and fresh clothing. The sooner this happened the better I'd feel.

From this point on, throughout France, I did not have the slightest idea where I was. We were constantly on the move. There were maps and orders so someone knew where we were. But after a while it didn't make a whole lot of difference. It was always the same: push the German army back towards their homeland. There were days when I felt I could conquer any obstacle, and other days I didn't want to move. I learned that a hero was nothing more than a soldier who was too frightened to be a coward. This never ceasing pace and vigilance, day after day, was starting to take its toll on all of us.

The Wounded

Corpses Everywhere

78

Chapter 13
Point Position

Traveling northeast, we headed across France towards Liege, Belgium to an engineering supply depot. There, we would pick up needed supplies and a few days' rest. That is, if we ever got there. It was three hundred miles away as the crow flies. We were zigzagging our way in vehicles and on foot through enemy infested countryside. This added both time and distance to our trek: not exactly a walk in the park!

In a division of twelve to fifteen thousand men, approximately two thousand five hundred did all the fighting. The rest were backup. They waited, watched, kept supplies moving and manned artillery. In my battalion and company, it worked much the same way. There were about three or four squads, twelve private riflemen, including myself, who were assigned to forward patrol or point and flank positions. Point is a lonely, dangerous position that took the brunt of most assaults. My buddies considered me lucky. I always got through unscathed when on patrol. I guess I just had a feel for it.

It was a cold, rainy, dismal morning. Rain dripped from my face as the wind buffeted my body. Muddy puddles were forming everywhere. I moved along methodically, carefully compensating for the unevenness of the stone studded road. My two flank men followed about twenty five to thirty yards back, fanned out as wide as the road, one on each side forming a triangle. Our objective was to penetrate sixteen miles deeper into enemy territory. The underbrush was thick so we stuck to the road. The secondary patrol group or squad was about one hundred to two hundred yards behind the flank. There were between fifty to one hundred men, depending on how safe headquarters thought it was. There were never enough men as far as I was concerned. The squad carried the radio, machine guns, bangalore tubes, bazookas, mine detectors and an assortment of other goodies. Point and flank positions always traveled with as little equipment as possible. The rest of my battalion could be a mile or two down the road past the squad. Artillery could be fifteen miles further. The squad would radio headquarters to report any activity, or to request artillery or air support when needed.

I moved up the road quickly and quietly, taking long smooth strides. I was a predator on the prowl, constantly pausing and crouching, scanning the area, using hand signals to the flank. We would be flushing out scattered pockets of Germans as we advanced. My senses had moved to maximum. I was ready to dole out death to whomever crossed my path. My flank always prepared to back me up. It's an uncomfortable feeling knowing death could strike at anytime, but I tried not to dwell on it. I was approaching a farm. As my jaw muscles tightened, broken thoughts raced through my mind. Was there an ambush up ahead or just some poor old farmer who gave up the ghost a long time ago and had no intention of fighting? One never knew, so I moved forward slowly and cautiously. More of the farm came into view. I could see a well at the rear of the building along with a fence. The side of the structure was thick with ivy. The front was in full view now. There was an uneasy silence in the air. I had a gut feeling that something was wrong. Slowly my finger tightened around the trigger. I sensed something near the edge of the woods. I squatted and raised my hand to signal my flank, when a shell arched overhead. With electrifying speed, I clutched my rifle firmly and dove for cover. I used the butt of my rifle to break my fall. There was an explosion and a crash of falling branches nearby. The shock wave slammed me into the ground, knocking my helmet off. Debris struck my neck and sifted down around me. I jerked my head up to spot the source of the attack. There was a smoldering hole uncomfortably close. Khaki colored toilet paper that I kept under the strap of my helmet was scattered all over. My head throbbed and ears rang. The squealing of pigs was coming from the barn. Bursts of machine gun fire rang out, pocking the ground all around me.

Without hesitation, I jammed my hands into the ground and scrambled up, retrieving my helmet and diving again, flattening myself on the road. I crawled towards the carcass of a dead horse as bullets whizzed overhead. It was better than trying to make it off the road to a ditch. The Germans loved to plant mines there. My flank had been returning fire but were out gunned in this fray. One cursed so loud I could hear him over the gunfire. My mouth was dry and my heart was beating at a frantic rate. I gulped air and tried to stay calm. My face and jacket were caked with mud, but otherwise I was okay. That is, if being sprawled behind a foul smelling dead horse in the rain and pinned down in a skirmish was okay! I could think of better situations I'd rather be in. Well, we were on patrol to shake up the enemy and we sure accomplished that! The wind rustled the trees and gunfire continued. I felt I was up the old proverbial creek. The irony was, my next moment could be my last and I was powerless to do anything but wait, just lie here silent as a stone and wait!

Lightning streaked across the sky as the rain slacked off. Suddenly, there were numerous bursts of gunfire from behind me. The squad had arrived, plastering the area mercilessly with machine gun fire and rifle grenades. I was stuck in the middle of a full scale fire fight, and then it happened. A murderous hail of artillery fire rained down on the enemy. The ground shook violently as this curtain of steel pulverized the landscape, brightening the cloudy day. I curled up holding my ears and prayed as the thunderous reverberations continued. Like the flick of a switch, it stopped. A quiet descended over the land. Columns of gray smoke ascended high above the shattered grove of trees. The enemy had been cut down! A radio call for artillery had ended the skirmish abruptly and decisively. The whole agonizing ordeal had taken less than fifteen minutes.

Up ahead was a grisly sight. Enemy dead were sprawled along the scarred road and field, looking more like piles of bloody rags than soldiers. Men writhed on the ground screaming in pain, knocking on death's door. There were badly mutilated bodies, pieces and parts everywhere. The ground was brightly stained with blood. A chill ran through my body, but for some reason I couldn't look away. I bit my bottom lip and swallowed hard as sweat beaded on my forehead. War's a cruel and ugly business.

We advanced the rest of the day without incident. By early evening, the countryside was calm and the horizon soft. It had been an arduous day. I was relieved to be back at headquarters. My reward was a dinner pail full of food and a good night's rest.

Many times the Germans let the forward patrol go through without firing. They would wait for the squad that followed before opening fire. Artillery and air strikes well in advance of our going out on patrol always made things easier. But indiscriminate bombings kill more than just the enemy. Many times we would find dead civilians and animals. It was not a pretty sight. I guess that was the price of war.

German prisoners complained that on every road and every field, all they saw was an endless stream of stinking American soldiers. We had become an unstoppable war machine!

Squad on Patrol

A Call for Artillery

On Target

Chapter 14
Tags and Mail

Now that my battalion was getting closer to Germany, I felt it was time to make a change for my own protection. Each soldier wears a metal identification tag, or dog tag, on a chain around his neck. One of the things listed on the dog tag is religion. Being Jewish, mine had the letter "H" for Hebrew. After hearing horror stories about what the Germans were doing to people of my religion, it behooved me to change it, in case of my capture. Headquarters had a small machine to make new dog tags should someone lose theirs. A few other men and I went down and got new tags made up, but this time they were stamped with a "C" for Catholic. It was one less thing I had to worry about.

Our outfit didn't function like most outfits. Groups of four or five of us could be gone from headquarters from anywhere from one day to three weeks. We would be assigned to help other companies in our sector, or sent out to set up temporary water supply stations. Whoever needed our help, for whatever job it was, we were available. Until we returned to headquarters, there was no mail and we had to eat C-rations and K-rations. C-rations were canned goods. K-rations were olive drab, cracker-jack size, wax coated boxes of dried food and an assortment of other things such as a four pack of cigarettes and a little packet of folded olive drab toilet paper. I kept the toilet paper behind a strap inside my helmet. Since I always had my helmet on, it was the best place to keep it. When I needed to go to relieve myself in the field, I took a shovel and dug a one foot deep trench, straddled it and squatted. When I finished, I filled in the trench. Hey, when someone had to go, he made do with whatever there was.

Mail came through pretty regularly, but only when we were back at headquarters. The trucks that delivered our food supplies also brought the mail. There was no question about my morale after mail call. I wore an ear to ear grin like a Cheshire cat. My fiancee always sent me letters and sometimes cookies. Cookies consistently brought looks of envy. She had baked them with her own little hands. Each one was wrapped individually in waxed paper and placed with tender loving care in a carton, then shipped all the way to Europe just for me. Eventually, I would get them. This one time, unbeknownst to me, she had placed personal little love notes in with some of cookies to surprise me. Boy, did I get a surprise! I received the carton and proceeded to pass some out to all my buddies. One of the guys got my love note. It said "here's my heart". The guy came back with the note and said "here Jack, you might want this. It's your girlfriend's heart". I was embarrassed, but it made for a good laugh. The guys ribbed me about it for days. I would just smile, raise my fist chest high, then raise my middle finger. I was very mature back then. I wrote to thank my fiancee for the cookies and asked her in a very nice way "please, no more love notes in the cookies", and explained what had happened. I'm sure she got a laugh out of it.

As long as I was traveling through France, I tried talking to some of the inhabitants. I found it very difficult to communicate because of my limited French and their limited English, but I gave it a shot anyway. I found them to be friendly, cordial people who appreciated that we were here.

It was hard to tell when we had left France and entered Belgium. To me, all road signs looked pretty much the same and the languages sounded similar. But nevertheless, I had made it in one piece. A few days more and I might even get some rest.

Chapter 15
The Bulge

With only a few more days of marching before we arrived at the engineer depot in Liege, Belgium, the weather took a turn for the worse. The air was damp and the temperature began plummeting. Heavy clouds were changing the color of the countryside as the wind picked up. Men's faces were heavy with fatigue as we pressed on, shoulders hunched against the wind. We all needed to rest, and soon.

It was bitter cold now, and a heavy snow was falling out of the slate gray sky. Ruts in the road were rapidly filling with frozen white flakes. A chill ran through my body as the snow pelted me, numbing my face. It clung to my clothing and crunched under foot, leaving impressions as I trudged on. We stopped for a brief break. I was shivering and felt wretched in my damp clothing. I leaned against a tree to shelter myself from the worst of the wind. Visibility had been reduced to nil. Nature had become another overwhelming, hostile obstacle. We regrouped and started out again, plunging forward through a storm towards our unseen destination.

By the time we arrived at the engineer depot, close to two feet of snow had fallen, but at least we made it in one piece. I was cold, dirty, tired and hungry. It had been about eight days since I last changed my clothes. I was smelling a little ripe and had been dreaming about a hot shower and a meal for two nights.

After being at the depot close to a week, we were well rested and fully re-supplied. The war was going well for our side. Our forces had already hammered the enemy all the way back to the heavily fortified Siegfried line, their own border. Allied Air Forces had achieved air superiority in the skies over Germany. There was a relentless bombing campaign being carried out. The British dropped their bombs after dark in a saturation raid. The American Flying Fortresses, escorted by the new Mustang fighters, attacked during the day with sophisticated precision bombings at specific targets. It looked as if by spring the war would be over in Europe. The American High Command was feeling a little complacent. Well, why not? We were the finest fighting force around, fighting for a righteous cause. Besides, it was nearly Christmas. But something kept nagging at my mind like an irritating fly. German prisoners had emphatically stated the Fuhrer was coming to visit the front around the sixteenth of December. They proudly stated "wait and see", as if they knew something we didn't. A few days later we realized the validity of their statements. High command had underestimated our opponent.

Hitler took the Allies by surprise as he launched a daring counterattack in the Ardennes. He had hoped to reverse his recent setbacks with a blistering assault of three armies of at least twenty divisions, which equated to more than three hundred fifty thousand men and tanks. His units plunged forward with alarming speed, buckling the entire American line, creating a large bulge sixty miles wide and fifty deep. Hence, this was named the Battle of the Bulge.

The Germans could not have asked for better weather conditions for an offensive. The sky was overcast so there would be no American air support. The temperature was twenty degrees and dropping. Two feet of snow blanketed everything. From the look of things, more was expected. This would certainly slow our response time. The Germans had one other advantage. They were fighting in close proximity to their own border. This meant short supply lines.

It had taken two full days before our Generals realized our army was losing men at an unbelievable rate. Orders came in to start moving different divisions to back up the line. The problem was, no such division existed anymore. Two of them had already been annihilated. We were losing the war! Men started to panic. No one knew what was happening. At that point, every available man was being thrown in to reinforce the line. My company headed southeast toward the enemy's strong point.

It was difficult terrain and weather conditions were horrendous. Trees were laden with ice and snow, their branches touched the ground. I was gazing out across a bleak, frigid, winter scene. My mood and spirit blended in perfectly. Only two days out, I saw trucks headed back loaded with dead Americans, their bodies stacked like logs. Now I was positive we were in big trouble. This could be the last road some of us would ever travel. We would certainly be separating the men from the boys.

Being a small combat engineer company, we had to advance cautiously. We had no real contact with infantry outfits on either side of us. If we pushed too fast and penetrated too deep, the Germans could come up from behind and engulf us. I did not even want to think about that scenario.

Not knowing how long I would be out in this harsh cold, I had put on almost every bit of clothing I owned. I wore two pair of pants, two shirts, a sweater and a field jacket which was topped off with a mackinaw. I managed a pair of galoshes over my boots and taped them against my pants to help keep snow out. Over my hands, I wore regular wool army gloves. Covering them, I had a pair of leather gloves. A band went around my wrist to secure them and keep snow out. It was difficult to hold my rifle and pull the trigger, but I had to protect my hands from the harsh winter elements. I also had a pair of wool mittens with a trigger finger, but I found that the wool slipped off the trigger, so I didn't use them. I was looking quite husky in all this clothing. Maneuvering was a lot harder, but it was certainly better than freezing to death.

I had been out about four days and the tempo of the snow had not changed. We were trying to keep up as steady a pace as was possible, through what was mostly fields. I was with a group of about one hundred and fifty men. A lot of them were my friends. Others I knew by sight. Without warning, a sudden explosion of gunfire erupted. I could hear the sputter of machine gun fire, as bullets whistle by. Men started slumping all around me, their bullet riddled bodies bent in unnatural positions. Instantly, the snow became a scarlet, spotted sheet. Panic seized me. Time seemed to be whirling in slow motion. I felt helpless. There was nothing I could do to help anyone. I knew if they weren't dead yet they would soon freeze to death. The cracking of gunfire echoed everywhere. Someone was barking orders, but in the momentary confusion I couldn't make them out. Suddenly, I felt nauseous. I became weak and lightheaded. My breath came in short bursts, as my chest heaved. My heart began to pound so loud it seemed to drown out everything around me. It all became a chaotic mass of light and sound. Closing my eyes a second allowed something inside of me to take over. Compressing my lips, I fired my rifle and met the attack head on. The deep snow made it hard to advance. I was laboring for breath, crawling and crouching for cover, moving on sheer instinct. I would do whatever it took to keep the pressure on the enemy. Men were moving in every direction. The German resistance was relentless and fanatical. Our advance continued but was measured in yards. Shells flew overhead sounding like freight trains. They shook the ground while still in the air. The battle smoke made the sky look black and stormy. The fighting was consistent right up until the long evening shadows began erasing all reality. Night, the first lull in the siege. This had been some day, a frigid hell! I'd seen men perform courageously, both individually and collectively, only to be shot down or blown to bits. I shuddered thinking about it.

Everyone held their positions. I had to keep moving in place to stay warm. I flattened the snow with my feet and backside. It crunched under the impact of my body as I shaped a hole to stand in and lean against. Fearing attack or freezing to death, I dared not fall asleep. A strange unnatural silence descended over the frigid black land. My teeth chattered and I shivered uncontrollably. Boy, I would have given anything for that lousy little pot bellied stove from the induction center. With my stomach starting to ache, I realized I had not eaten or drunk anything thing since the start of the day. I leaned back against the lip of the hole and had myself a K-ration. Dry cereal with powdered milk, powdered lemonade and a rectangular shaped cracker we called a dog biscuit because of its texture, were the only rations not frozen. I washed it all down by eating snow because my canteen was also frozen solid. What a gourmet meal that was.

Snow started falling again. I sat in my little hole and kept wiggling from side to side to stay warm. The wind whipped the snow, swirling it around me, dusting my body. I held my rifle ready to fire, but only as a last resort. Firing in the darkness produced a bright muzzle flash that would lead the enemy right to my position. I knew they were out there somewhere. I could feel their presence. As time passed, my rifle was feeling much heavier. My arms ached in protest. Blinded by darkness, paranoia rocketed in. My imagination became a machine that I couldn't turn off. I would only die once, but the fear of death was always lingering. To kill or be killed was always just a second away. For all I knew, the entire German army was moving in on me! I fought desperately to regain control of my thoughts. I needed to keep my mind occupied or I'd go mad. I began playing little mental games, one of which was recalling the full names of the men I had met since enlisting in the army. This also helped me stay awake. Even though my mind was preoccupied, my hearing remained extremely acute. The silent darkness made that easy.

The first light of day brought a view of horror. Dead American soldiers lay frozen in awkward positions, their open mouths filled with snow. It was an unbelievable mind numbing scene. I closed my eyes and rubbed my temples as my mind raced. Clenching my fists, I tried hard to blank the images from my mind and maintain self control. Moments later, gunfire erupted forcing me to change my focus.

The savage fighting had raged on for three days now and casualties were high. Nighttime never offered much relief. I had to fight the bitter cold, which was becoming more difficult without enough sleep or food. I resorted to eating powdered lemonade and snow all day to help quench both my thirst and hunger. It was so sour it made my mouth pucker and my body shudder.

I had no idea how far I had walked or where I was, and at this point, I didn't much care. I was barely going through the motions. The one thing I knew for sure, was at this rate, I wasn't going to last much longer. Having already lost the feeling in my feet, I was finding it hard to walk under the weight of my equipment. As the cold air burned my lungs, I was becoming lightheaded and oblivious to my surroundings.

Sometime during the later part of that third day, the storm broke. The weather changed dramatically and American air strikes began. A smile came to my tired face as swarms of planes swooped in at treetop level strafing and bombing, laying down a wall of steel and shrapnel, rolling the enemy back.

Trucks were sent in to pull us out, and none too soon! Out of the group of one hundred and fifty or so men that I started out with, only twenty one of us were still standing. Most of them just stared off into the distance. Their eyes looked empty, their faces as if carved from clay. Some were stippled in blood. This horrific experience was etched into my brain for life. Miraculously, I had escaped death, but I had friends who weren't as lucky. Their bodies wouldn't be found until spring, when the snow melted.

Chapter 16
The Hospital

With my feet no longer able to support me, a soldier had to assist me as I hobbled over to one of the trucks that were sent in to pull us out. It was a long, bumpy ride to some sort of field hospital. I presumed it was somewhere in Belgium. The first order of things was to wrap us in blankets and give us hot coffee. My hands trembled as I raised the cup to my lips. Fear was visible on everyone's faces. No one really considers how much they want to live, until they might die. Next, the nursing staff helped us remove our boots and then, the rest of our badly stained and dirty clothing. This turned out to be a nightmare come true for some of the men. Frostbite! It was so bad in some cases that their feet had turned completely black and gave off a foul stench. Amputation needed to be done immediately. My feet were frozen and were starting to hurt like hell. They had frostbite damage although it was not that severe. I guess wearing those galoshes over my boots paid off. I was moved to a ward where I was helped into a bed. This bed felt soft, warm and comfortable. I was finding it hard to tell if the illumination were poor or my eyes were failing from lack of sleep. I closed my eyes and instantly sank into a deep sleep as if weighted down by a ton of boulders. The next thing I knew, I was waking from a twenty four hour snooze. Boy, how time flies when your having fun.

I had the world's worst taste in my mouth. After a week or so of not having washed, I couldn't have smelled much better either. I must have been a haggard, frightful sight. As I moved I winced. The ache resonated through every fiber of my body. My feet throbbed as if they had been hit with a hammer, a large, heavy hammer! For quite a while, the pain seemed almost unendurable. This brought a sudden worry to mind. I quickly pulled back the cover to check if my feet had been amputated. This brought an instant sigh of relief. Then another ache hit me, my stomach! I wanted food! Right then and there I knew I was going to be okay, but only if I could get someone to bring me food. When they finally brought my food, I ate as if I were racing against the clock. I had to remind myself to slow down, take human bites, and taste the food.

Spending two more days in the hospital helped me recuperate. I met an officer who, like me, was from New York. He was a military dentist and had also been a dentist before the war. He was assigned to help out in the hospital because of the enormous amount of wounded coming in from the Battle of the Bulge. This soldier was a saint! He spent hours talking with me and massaging my feet back to health.

I had ample time to catch up on my letter writing. There I sat, pen in hand and a ear to ear smile on my face. It felt good to clear my mind of all its ghosts. Receiving letters from home was another powerful factor in keeping my spirits up. I would read them over and over while unconsciously playing with the chain around my neck that held my dog tags. Oh, how sweet those letters were!

The estimates of dead and wounded Americans were staggering. One hundred fifty thousand was the number circulating through the hospital wards. That represented about ten divisions. Hospitals from France to the United States were filled with American soldiers. The estimates of the number of German dead and wounded were double. Thank God we won that battle.

There was also a story circulating about some American paratroopers being pinned down and encircled by five German divisions in a strategically located city called Bastogne. They were calling these soldiers "The battered bastards of Bastogne". Everyday, the Germans would relay a message demanding their surrender. The American general in command would give a defiant reply of "Fuck you, send us more Germans to kill." He did this knowing his troops were grossly outnumbered and running out of ammunition and other supplies. The weather had prevented American planes from dropping supplies. If it weren't for these guys holding out against savage enemy attacks for nine days, we might have lost the Battle of the Bulge. Later, news reports of the incident relayed that Brigadier General McAuliffe had answered the Germans defiantly, but had said "NUTS". I tended to believe what I had heard in the hospital. It was a little more realistic, although "nuts" did sound nicer for the American public.

The tide had finally turned. Technically, the battle was over in France and Belgium. Now, it would begin in Germany. There would never be another counterattack like this again.

Chapter 17
Aachen

From the hospital I was sent back to my outfit, which was being regrouped. Waiting for replacements from the United States took time. The trouble was, we were getting raw recruits with only six weeks of training. No one in my company was thrilled with this. We needed seasoned troops!

General Dwight D. Eisenhower had issued an order that every private who participated in the Battle of the Bulge be promoted to Private First Class. It was considered a battlefield promotion. My pay was going from fifty dollars a month to a whopping fifty four dollars, plus ten percent overseas pay. We joked about our pay, saying that the army was giving us one dollar a body to kill Germans.

Advancing on the heels of the retreating Germans, the City of Aachen was our next stop. Aachen was the first German city to fall. The American First Army had dispatched a "surrender or die" ultimatum to the German garrison in Aachen. No reply was received. They had elected to fight. Aachen, formerly with a population of one hundred sixty five thousand, was completely pulverized by bombings and artillery. After more than a week of fierce street battles, the main Nazi defenders withdrew, but not until the city had been destroyed.

At last, fighting was on German soil. This put our infantry close to the industrial Ruhr, one of the principal citadels of Germany's armed might. My battalion headed for Aachen, using the main autobahn. I was in my six by six truck manning the fifty caliber machine gun at the head of the convoy. A jeep was the only vehicle in front of me. After an hour or two, the convoy slowed and turned right, off the main autobahn. We followed a two lane paved road for quite a few miles. This turned into a rutted gravel and dirt road. Rocks popped and crunched beneath the truck as it bounced along. The road widened and curved to the left, revealing the entrance of the city. We moved forward a few hundred yards more, slowly coasting to a stop. The driver cut the engine and pulled up the hand brake. There wasn't a sound to be heard except for the tick of hot metal from the trucks, nor a soul in sight. Columns of dark smoke towered from row after row of flattened chalky-gray buildings that contrasted sharply against the bright blue sky. There were no trees or vegetation to be seen anywhere, just steep piles of broken rubble, earth and rock littering the area. Massive bomb craters could be seen everywhere. There was nothing but a shell where a city had once stood. The city's center had literally been leveled to the ground. I took a deep breath. The air was thick with the scent of burnt debris. Never had I seen such total destruction. I quickly glanced at my watch before getting out of the truck. We would probably be here a while waiting for tanks with bulldozer blades to come up and clear the streets. Keeping the army moving was one of our main functions. The speed of the advance largely depended on us. Engineers go under, over or through anything. This time we had to shove it out of the way. I climbed out of the truck, took my helmet off and cradled it under my arm. My head could use the fresh air. Everyone was standing in groups outside the trucks talking, smoking and joking around. I took my glasses off to remove a smudge. Suddenly, my ears picked up the unmistakable high whine of a rapidly approaching plane. Putting my glasses on, I looked upward as a sickening feeling enveloped me. Shading my eyes from the sun, my gaze moved across the terrain. Suddenly, it appeared in my field of vision. A lone plane was silhouetted against the horizon. I made a mad dash for my truck. Our convoy was stopped dead in the road with nowhere to move. We were like a bunch of sitting ducks at a shooting gallery. The plane spotted us and was diving in at treetop level for a strafing run. There was a moment of bedlam as men scrambled in every direction to get to their trucks or dive for cover. I was the first man up on a truck and could hear the plane's guns pounding away at us. I pulled back the bolt on my machine gun and was first to return fire. I craned my neck to see, as it swooped over my head spitting bursts of metal and fire. I could feel the turbulence as it made its pass. With my sights locked on the plane, I swung my machine gun around, following its flight path, leaving a trail of fiery tracers. I scored a hit! Chunks of the plane's tail came splintering away. By this time, there was the ear splitting sound of every gun opening up down the convoy line. The sky was a criss-cross of arching tracer light, glaring and quickly disappearing. It was like a fireworks show on the Fourth of July. The plane banked sharply to the left, climbed, and headed for the mountains. I suppose not carrying any bombs and facing such fierce resistance forced the lone plane to call off its attack. Luckily, the convoy suffered no loss of life and sustained very little damage. I patted my machine gun in appreciation and slumped down into the cab of the truck. I had gripped the gun so tightly my hands were red. I took a deep breath and let it out slowly. I needed to unwind.

A short time later, I sat perched on the top of the truck, watching the tanks rumble forward with their bulldozer blades attached. They began smashing a path through the city so the convoy could proceed again. I jumped down into the cab next to the driver, who was napping. My jumping into the cab startled him. A letter fell from his hand, onto the seat. I picked it up and handed it back to him with my apologies. He just nodded. The order was given to move out. The driver turned on the ignition and the engine roared. A blue plume of smoke poured out the exhaust pipe. He put the truck in gear, released the hand brake and we began to move forward. We filed through the shattered streets as we made our way towards the main road. Our next stop was the city of Julich.

Chapter 18
Julich

The city of Julich was only about twenty miles away, as darkness began descending over the country-side like a large blanket. This meant I would be moving on foot soon. Our objective was to get to Julich, so there would be no stopping until we got there. It was pitch black now. Looking up, I saw only faint stars. The moon had disappeared behind dark clouds. Quietly, we began advancing on foot across what seemed to be a freshly plowed field. We had to make sure it was safe for the trucks to travel on. There were about a dozen of us fanned out walking in a straight line. I slipped on something soft that gave off a foul odor. A sudden gust of wind rustled some trees nearby. I heard the snap of a branch up ahead. We all froze in our tracks. Some-where out in front of me in that dreadful darkness, I could scarcely make out muffled footsteps. I strained to hear over the pounding of my heart as I raised my rifle. But shooting into this black abyss could mean disaster. I stood still as a statue. Sweat dripped from my face and trickled down my back. I waited. The footsteps started again. My eyes stared deep into the darkness, desperately searching for an identifiable target. The footsteps continued, getting closer and closer. Death could be seconds away! Now I could hear a faint breathing. How much longer could I wait to fire? Should I let them make the first move? A moment later gunshots ripped through the silence. I flinched. There was a loud thud just to the left of me. Someone down the line had let loose. There was silence again. No one moved or said a word. Seconds ticked off like hours, but no return gunfire erupted. A few feet to the left of me, there was the unmistakable metallic click of a cigarette lighter. The flame revealed a huge dead cow lying in a pool of blood in front of us. Immediately, we burst into a laughter of relief. It turned out we had crossed a cow pasture and had some serious boot cleaning to do. I hope someone was going to come back in the morning and butcher that cow. I sure could go for a fat juicy steak, although I don't think the farmer that owned the cow was going to be very happy.

I was back in my truck staring blankly through the dirty windshield as traces of smoke blew across the morning sky. A bird flew past with something long and fleshy dangling from its beak. I thought about all the other scavengers that were out there foraging and feasting on dead soldiers. My body stiffened as my stomach heaved. Shutting my eyes a few second allowed the feeling to pass.

Dawn had brought a new day and a fresh view of devastation. Gray-gutted structures that lacked definition, and a decimated landscape, sat in silent testimony to the intensity of the bombing the city had received. Even the snow had a gray tint. The only things moving were some papers turning cartwheels across the rubble. Meeting little resistance somehow made the view a little more palatable. So far we'd been lucky, but how long would our luck hold out?

We cleared the way through the city and headed for our next objective. Duren was twenty miles southeast of here, and we were headed straight for it.

Chapter 19
Duren

The ride to Duren was a slow and bumpy one. The day had been uneventful until we reached the outskirts of the city. The German army had deserted but needed time to make their escape. They did this by digging a long trench across the road and one hundred yards or so into the fields on each side. The trench was filled with children (Hitler youth) and elderly men, all fully armed to defend their town and slow us down. I didn't like the idea of killing children and old men, but this was a war and they were in that trench waiting to kill us. Sitting behind me was a half mile long convoy of men, tanks and equipment. It was lined up like some huge freight train ready to move forward. There was no slowing us down.

Crouching low, we surveyed our target. This was going to be a turkey shoot. Normally, trenches were dug in a zigzag shape with mines placed at either end. This way, if it were flanked, everyone in it wouldn't be exposed to gunfire. The Germans, in their hasty retreat, made this trench straight and probably neglected to place mines on each side, making it vulnerable to flank attack. Two teams of men moved into the field on either side of the trench, while a third team began laying down a barrage of gunfire in a frontal assault. The trench resistance was weak and disorganized. My group moved through the field with the help of a mine detector, just in case. We also had two men with flame throwers. We charged forward, striking with the speed of a rattlesnake. The men with the flame throwers blasted the ditch at point blank range, pouring in an inferno of liquid flame. Sheets of fire leaped from the trench. I was breathing hard. I crouched low in readiness to direct cover fire into the opening. It was never necessary. Anguished screams, shrieks, shrills and choked cries rang out as the sea of suffocating flames seared their bodies. Black billows of smoke gushed skyward. I felt the intense heat and saw flames shimmer in men's eyes. Charred figures staggered in agony, until the consuming flames brought them withering to the ground. The bizarre horror momentarily froze my body in place. The unmistakable vile stench of burnt flesh cascaded over me, jolting me back to reality, and what a reality it was. There was nothing remaining but roasted, grotesquely disfigured corpses. The battlefield had become a crematory. I stood there staring, my body one big knot. I whipped the sweat from my face and moistened my lips. I realized I hadn't even fired a shot. Looking at others, I saw my pain reflected in their faces. Some men looked abnormally pale.

It took only minutes for bulldozers to fill in the scorched trench and cover the remains, then compact it down. While looking at the spot where the trench had been, I bit my bottom lip. It was hard to believe there was no sign of what had just happened only moments ago. Almost like it had all been a bad dream.

We moved through the city, clearing the last of the enemy holdouts. Camp was set up outside of the city. While sitting and talking with some of the men from my company, someone from headquarters came over and notified four of us that we were being signed out to set up a temporary water supply station in a city called Koblenz, about sixty miles southeast of here. I wondered what peril tomorrow would bring.

Surveying the Target

Chapter 20
Koblenz

It was sunrise and time to pick up mimeographed maps of the area. A mimeographed copy had a blue, purple color and a strong alcohol smell. The army called them ditto maps. This was what was used before copy machines. A topographical engineer made the maps. The temporary water station was to be located next to a brewery. My entire face became one big smile. This certainly could be interesting! Having no idea how long we would be gone, we loaded our truck and brought along a few loaves of bread and plenty of C-rations. John, who was from Texas, was the name of one of the men in my group who spoke German. This would help once we got to Koblenz.

The air was crisp and the sky clear as we made our way towards our destination. With the windows open and the heat on full blast, we sat cramped in the front seat with our rifles facing muzzle up between our legs. I turned up the collar of my coat to block the wind. I became fascinated by the beauty and contour of the land as we drove by. It reminded me of home. Too bad we were at war. This looked like a nice place to visit.

It took us a few hours to get to Koblenz and only a few minutes to locate the brewery. We just followed the scent of beer. We all climbed out of the truck stretching and glancing around. I took a few steps back and forth to limber my legs. One had fallen asleep and was tingling. We headed straight for the front door of the brewery. A large wooden sign hung directly above it. I had no idea what it said, it was in German. We walked in with a live and let live attitude. All we wanted was the use of their water. I was sure no one wanted any trouble. They would probably want to get us in and out of their lives as soon as possible. John asked to speak to the owner or whoever was in charge. A big, round, friendly looking man with blue eyes, red cheeks and blonde hair came over, offering his hand to each of us. In a deep hearty voice he told us this was a family owned business and because he was the oldest son he was in charge. I studied the man a moment and noticed he was wide eyed, and his gait was unsteady. It looked to me as if he had been sampling his wares. Not only was this man agreeable about the water, but he was also willing to provide us with a place to stay for the duration. A worker was told to bring us over to meet the occupants of the house, which was only three doors away from the brewery. It was a good sized house that had a family of four living in it, a husband and wife with two children. The second we entered, the smell of food enveloped us. The aroma made my mouth water. In the kitchen, a large pot was simmering on the stove. Nearby on a table was a cutting board and knife with the remnants of chopped food. The man was tall and thin, with dark hair, mustache and a gaunt face. The woman was short and plain looking with a mole above her upper lip. She was wearing a yellow house dress that had seen better days. The girl was fifteen and the boy was younger. A small skinny dog with short brown fur and floppy ears appeared from behind them. It sniffed at our boots and ran off. The man, who was also an employee at the brewery, showed us a room all four of us would share. We would also have access to the kitchen and bathroom. Soaking in a hot tub came right to mind. It had been over a year since I last had a hot bath. Everyone in the house was able to speak a little English. This would make living in the house that much easier. The room had a dark brown plank floor and was furnished with a square table and two comfortable looking wooden chairs with high backs. A picture hung on the far wall next to a window with dark blue curtains. There was ample room to place our four wooden, canvas cots. We would use our sleeping bags on top of the cots. This room looked palatial compared to some of the places in which I had already slept.

Late that afternoon, outside the brewery, we set up a three thousand gallon canvas water tank. I ran a fire hose into the brewery and hooked it up to their water line. I went back outside and connected the hose to the gasoline driven water pump. I started the engine while the others finished connecting the one hundred pound purification filtering system. The hose from the filtering system was thrown over the top of the tank and we started pumping water. We looked at each other and gave a thumbs up sign. By the time the tank was full, darkness had crept over the land. Trucks wouldn't start arriving for water until morning, so we were done for the day. We went back into the brewery to disconnect our fire hose. John went over to one of the workers to talk to him. They both went outside and returned moments later with a five gallon jerry can from our truck. The worker proceeded to fill it with beer. John tipped the man with some cash and saluted him. We scrambled over and helped John carry the can back to our newfound living quarters. John informed us that the worker would fill the can every day if we wanted. Our job would be to empty it each night. Oh boy, were we in for whopping hangovers! This was sweet tasting dark beer with a low alcohol content. It was the first time I ever had any and the more I drank the sweeter it got. I wasn't use to drinking, so low alcohol or not, its effects hit me quick, and made walking and talking a parallel adventure.

Morning came way too soon. Sunlight filled the room through the frosted window and hit me like a hammer right between the eyes. I inched my head over to the window and leaned my face against it to peer outside. When my eyes finally focused, I could see that the ground was white with frost. It reminded me of a Christmas card I had seen. Two birds landed on the window ledge and began fighting for territory. My breath condensed on the window and blurred my view. I glanced at my watch. It was almost six o'clock and time to drag myself out of bed. We had to prepare for the trucks that would be coming for water. Breakfast didn't much appeal to me today, so right after washing up, I went to the kitchen, grabbed a cup of black coffee and headed for the brewery. I sat outside a while taking slow, savoring sips of the warm brew, hoping it would help clear my grogginess. When I went into the brewery, the smell hit me hard. My stomach turned upside down and my head started spinning, or maybe my head was spinning from the night before. Either way, I felt like a dog that had just been kicked down a flight of stairs head first. Well, I would just have to bite the bullet. There was work to be done.

We spent the better part of the day pumping water and filling trucks. Later that afternoon, we went back to the house, had a light meal and went right to sleep. From that point on, we abandoned the idea of finishing off five gallons of beer every night.

The days that followed were great. At the end of each day we spent time in the town shops and talked to some of the residents. Back at the house, we experimented in the kitchen. Crossing our fingers, we mixed a concoction of C-rations and food we had bought, hoping for the best. What a surprise! It was edible. It's obvious we didn't have very sophisticated palates. It was almost like being on a vacation. Well, at least there was no killing or taking orders. Hell, we always knew what had to be done and we did it! I wish I could have sat out the rest of the war right here. The most fun I had in the army was between battles. But sadly, there were more battles to be fought until this damn war was over.

After ten wonderful days, reality reared its ugly head again. Someone from headquarters was sent to tell us to shut down our operation and head back. Headquarters was on the move and so were we. We were to meet up with H & S Company about eighteen miles outside the city of Cologne. There we would receive new orders. We unhappily packed our things, which included a five gallon can of beer, and said our good-byes. Within two hours we were on the road.

Chapter 21
The Wall

As we made our way to the rendezvous point, we saw demolished German tanks strewn across the country side. They had been reduced to nothing more than torn and twisted charred hulks of metal. Some of the crippled metal monsters were still smoldering. Upon our return to headquarters, we found that we were being signed out the next day. Someone else in the sector needed our help. At dawn, we were to travel sixteen miles west to the outskirts of some small town to assist the 250th artillery group. I guess it was just the luck of the draw that we got this assignment. At least it was only for one day, so it wouldn't be necessary to pack many supplies.

First light brought an ominous sky. After picking up our map from headquarters, we jumped in our truck and headed out. Due to the sudden thaw, we were maneuvering down a slick, slushy road that was rapidly becoming a sea of mud. The truck's tires churned steadily through the slippery mess as a dense fog and misty rain rolled in. This was just great! Now, we were navigating through pea soup. I was sure glad I wasn't the driver. We crawled along at a snail's pace. At times, the rain drummed down on the windshield so hard the wipers couldn't keep up. It felt like it took forever, but we did finally find the artillery group. Actually, we heard the deafening crashes of their cannons and followed the sound. The fog cleared and the rain tapered to a drizzle. Sitting only a dozen yards away were big one hundred fifty five millimeter cannons. Their barrels were raised skyward pumping out shells at a frantic rate, shaking the ground we drove on. They sounded like giant jackhammers, as their shells hacked away at stubborn cores of resistance. The air was heavy with the smell of gunpowder, and shell casings littered the ground behind the cannons. Artillery shells were being fired so rapidly that captured Germans had said they thought we had developed an automatic artillery cannon.

We parked our truck and walked over to find the officer in command. Our assignment was to carry the empty one hundred fifty five millimeter shell casings that were lying behind the cannons and bring them to another location. Then, we were to stack them up in neat piles so they could be packed up and shipped back to the States. Casings were quite valuable because they were made of brass. This enabled them to be put back into dies and reused. Gloves were given to us to help protect our hands while doing the job. Some of the shells would still be hot from being fired. We each grabbed a shell casing and headed for the streets looking for a place we could stack them. I would say the shells weighed about seven pounds, were one and a half foot long and about eight inches in diameter. We carried them about two blocks. Using a building to support the casings, we began stacking them up. We worked for an hour and agreed it was time to take a break. We jumped up and sat on the top of the pile of casings. Ted, who was from Pennsylvania, was a stocky man with curly hair, large callused hands and a hot temper. With an intense look in his eyes, he shook a cigarette out of a pack and wedged it between his lips. Ted chain smoked Lucky Strike cigarettes. Lighting it, be blew a cloud of blue-gray smoke, then waved it away with his hand. A moment later his anger flared. Seething, he shouted, "we're nothing but slave labor!", as the cigarette wagged in his mouth. He certainly wasn't going to get an argument out of me. He jumped down off the shells and began pacing. Then he yelled, "this is a bull shit, back breaking job." We all agreed with him and decided to make the work a little easier on ourselves by making one large stack of shell casings instead of multiple stacks down the block. Screw anybody who didn't like it! Ted flicked his cigarette on the ground and snuffed it out with the tip of his boot. Ted looked drained, but everyone I knew in this war looked exhausted and miserable. At least, now, we had a goal: to build the largest stack of shell casings the 250th Artillery Group had ever seen.

By the end of the day, we had a pile that was over seven feet high and ran between two buildings, completely blocking the street and making it totally impossible for anyone to pass by. It was our artistic version of the Great Wall of China. An officer with a jagged scar on his left cheek came over to inspect our job. Based on his demeanor, he was not amused. With his arms raised and flailing, and his face bright red, he shouted in complete exasperation, "what the hell!" There was a long moment of awkward silence. It took everything we had to suppress our laughter and keep straight faces, but we somehow managed. Completely flabbergasted, the officer shouted "dismissed!" and dispatched us back to our headquarters. From the sound of his voice, we knew not to waste any time getting out of this place. All I know is, we had the best side splitting laugh on the drive back to headquarters.

Artillery

126

Artillery Shells

Chapter 22
Cologne

Along the Rhine River, the Nazis were withdrawing in frantic confusion to the east bank and destroying their bridges in their wake. It would be our job to build new ones.

Twenty five large scale aerial attacks had taken place spreading some forty thousand tons of bombs on the City of Cologne. Hearing numbers like that stunned me. I couldn't even imagine what that amount of bombs looked like. Two thirds of the once beautiful city had been utterly destroyed. A large cathedral was the only building still standing and not severely damaged. That was an uncanny sight. I stopped a moment and thought about my own faith, and said a silent prayer. With the fall of Cologne, all of the west bank of the Rhine River to the north, with the exception of small pockets, were being brought under our control. South of Cologne, American units were closing in on the river and the city of Bonn.

Neither natural barriers nor man made obstacles could stop our forward motion. The enemy was being pushed back across their last defense line, the Rhine River.

The 1285th, my battalion, had been sent to Cologne to help build a floating pontoon bridge across the Rhine. The 283rd Engineer Battalion was here already and had started building, but was having trouble because of its unfamiliarity with the class forty floating Bailey bridge. My battalion was fully trained in this bridge class. Company B and C would build it for them. Men would scout ahead to survey the bank of the river and clear it of any mines. This job was dangerous for two reasons: one was sniper fire, the other was the accidental detonation of a mine. This bridge would be named in honor of Captain Victor J. Vega, who lost a leg to a mine while on the east bank of the river. The bridge was being built near the remains of the old Hohenzolleren Bridge. The length of our bridge would reach one thousand two hundred ninety feet. The center section would rise above the water without supports. The bridge was built in a fraction of the time it would have taken using normal construction practices. We accomplished this while constantly be exposed to enemy gunfire. Thousands of American troops, trucks and tanks lined up nose to tail waiting for us to finish. Not since 1805, when Napoleon's forces had swept across the Rhine, had the Rhine been crossed by an invading army. The second the bridge was completed our troops began pouring across the river. There were hundreds of refugees and prisoners waiting to cross in the other direction. We had to place men with walkie-talkies on each side of the bridge to direct traffic since it was only wide enough to allow the flow to go in one direction. Troops, tanks and supplies always had top priority. Supplies also meant hot meals and mail were on their way. Between battles, there were usually large lapses of time. This gave us a chance to read and write letters, shower, shave and wash our clothes.

Our army had captured the Ludendorff Bridge at Remagen and had established a bridgehead at the Rhine. This vital bridge was seized just as the Germans desperately tried to blow it up. American troops crossed it under heavy gunfire and succeeded in widening and strengthening the bridgehead.

Our army was moving so fast that the front was more than one hundred miles in advance of headquarters. Because of this, high command didn't always receive up to date information on what was going on at the front. At Remagen, they never knew our troops had made it to the other side of the Rhine. It wasn't in their plans for our army to cross at this point. I had heard that Lieutenant General Omar N. Bradely was so mad he got right on his field radio and called the command center. He asked something to the effect of, "what would you like us to do, go back across the Rhine because its not on your map?" Well, they had their problems, and I had mine, staying alive.

Mine Detector

Captain Vega Bridge

Our Sign

Chapter 23
The Map

A temporary water supply station was needed and my group was given the assignment. We picked up provisions, ditto maps of the area and our equipment. It all got loaded on the truck and we were on our way. According to calculations, we should have been able to find the location of a small stream in about two hours.

Almost four hours had passed and still no stream. I was perplexed! Maps rustled in the cab of the truck as we rechecked our coordinates. This time, I noticed some of the lines on the map were unclear, making the map difficult to read. Just my luck! Regardless, I felt it couldn't be much further, so we just continued on our present course. The dirt road became narrow and winding, with many deep ruts. It got so narrow in places that the brush and tree branches were scraping the sides of the truck. The road curved sharply to the left and we headed downhill. The air had the sweet smell of a forest. The springs squeaked as the truck bobbed up and down through the potholes, making clouds of dust. Except for the noise the truck was making, it was quiet and peaceful out here. Daylight was running out and we were desperate to find this stream. At the bottom of the hill, the road opened up and led to a clearing that was right next to a stream. Hallelujah! The map was just a bit off, but this looked about right. We jumped out of the truck, slamming the doors closed. It was already dark, but we could see an encampment a few hundred yards away on the other side of the stream. We had no idea who they were and it wasn't our job to know. We had work to be done and began unloading the truck and setting up the equipment to start pumping water into the three thousand gallon water tank. We were too busy to visit the other camp, but come morning, we would go over to see if we could get some real food instead of eating our "tasty rations". A full moon gave us just enough light to work. I adjusted the carburetor chock on the gasoline driven water pump and pulled the starter rope. The engine just coughed. Yanking the rope two more times caused it to sputter and start. This engine made some racket, especially out in the open. If the soldiers in the other camp didn't know we were here before, they sure did now.

The night air was cold, clear and fresh. I could see my breath. Dampness seemed to rise up from the frosted ground, chilling my body. The cold was offset by the hot glowing coals of our campfire. A log popped, crackled and hissed as it broke and rolled. This created an entertaining shower of red and yellow sparks that surged skyward. We opened a few cans of rations for a quick dinner. I saluted the others with my canteen and took a drink. I wiped my mouth on my sleeve. It always doubled as a napkin. Posting a watch tonight wouldn't be necessary because the other camp was so close by. Besides, seasoned troops slept well even with death lurking about, and we were nowhere near the enemy. I looked out across the land at the distant pinpoints of light. The moon peered from behind a cloud and lit the tops of the black trees, as a cold breeze rustled their branches. I lay back and drifted off to sleep.

There is nothing like someone pulling on my jacket at five in the morning to bring me bolt upright from a deep sleep. Disoriented and eyes blinking rapidly, I fumbled for my rifle. A few deep breaths cleared my head. I ran my fingers through my hair and rubbed my face as I jumped to my feet. The day was dawning with the sky a red glow. I squinted tensely at my buddy saying, "What's up?" He was white faced, eyes darting and breathing hard. He pointed towards the other camp, cleared his throat and in a panicky voice said, "The soldiers in the other camp aren't wearing the same shape helmets as us!" Fragmented thoughts raced through my mind. I was trying to comprehend and assimilate what he had just said. Germans? How was it possible? I shook my head in dismay and disbelief. The map! My jaw muscles tightened as I shouted, "the Goddamn map!" The words seem to just hang in the air. The men looked at me quizzically. I explained that a misprint on the map had led us behind enemy lines. Boy, someone screwed this one up royally! Since we were not supposed to be in enemy territory, we hadn't brought along our fifty caliber machine gun. Three of us had M1 rifles, rifle grenades and a few hand grenades. The sergeant only had a carbine. There seemed to be at least twenty to thirty soldiers in the other camp but we weren't sure. We were in big trouble! Then again, maybe not. The Germans knew we were here but must have thought we were Germans, just like we thought they were Americans. Besides, this was no time to get into a fire fight being that we were outnumbered, and had no idea how the Germans were armed. If we could get out of here before the sun rises we still had a chance. In a frenzy, we quietly packed the truck with what we could. The full water tank was staying right where it sat. There was no time to empty it. Hell, let them drink the water. We all jumped into the truck and headed up the road at full speed. Gravel crunched and popped beneath the truck, as it bucked violently. I was lifted clear out of my seat, my helmet banging the top of the truck's cab. Things were falling off the truck and twice we almost skidded off the road, once nearly missing a tree. By the time we reached the crest of the hill, we felt we had put enough distance between us and the camp, so we slowed our pace. The whole way back I was fuming. All I could think about was getting my hands around the throat of the son of a bitch who screwed up the map, almost getting us captured or killed.

Chapter 24
Dusseldorf

My battalion was headed northwest following the Rhine River. The next bridge to be built was at Dusseldorf, but first we had to make our way through four other cities: Rheydt, Monchen Gladback, Viersen and Neuss. When we reached Dusseldorf, there was still house to house street fighting going on. The enemy kept trying to make a line of resistance. Our constant, powerful surge forward was pushing them east and preventing this from happening.

As we entered the city, I turned to see a German soldier running up the block. He stopped to hurl a hand grenade. That was his first and last mistake. A solitary American soldier about fifty feet in front of me acted instinctively. Without breaking stride, he brought his rifle up in one swift, graceful movement, letting loose with several bursts, instantly chopping the German down.

The American soldier just nodded his head in satisfaction, and continued on.

During house to house fighting, we used a lot of hand grenades. When we suspected the enemy was hiding in a room, we tossed a grenade in rather than take the chance of a confrontation in a confined area. Room to room searches needed to be done in all the apartment buildings to rout out snipers. I hated this kind of search, not that I liked the others any better. There was never enough room to maneuver, and danger could be lurking in every room. It was not only enemy soldiers I feared, but the booby traps as well. The Germans placed them everywhere.

The buildings in the area were gray with soot, robbing them of their former luster. Six of us entered a corner, five story apartment building. We split into three groups and advanced into a dimly lit, narrow hallway. The place had a musty odor. My eyes glanced down one side of the hall and up the other. There was a row of doors, some opened, some closed. Peeling plaster hung from the ceiling. It gave the place an eerie, haunted look. It reminded me of the fun house at Coney Island, but this wasn't fun! There was a loud crunch under my boot. My body went rigid, my heart raced. Looking down at the floor, I saw broken glass. I exhaled hard in relief and continued on. My partner glanced at me. His face was tense and sweaty. I gestured with my head towards the first opened door. My partner followed my gaze and flanked the door. We craned our necks to peer around the door jamb, then jumped in, rifles ready. The room was in shambles. Pictures on the wall leaned left and right. Books and papers were strewn on the floor, as if left there in a hurry. Chunks of plaster from the ceiling and walls were mingled among the mess. A large book laying on the floor attracted my attention. I scooped it up and shoved it under my coat to keep as a souvenir. I still have that book to this day. We moved into a bedroom. My partner held his rifle ready as I yanked open the first closet door. It was empty except for some wooden hangers on the floor. I moved to the next closet. Something caught my eye as I pulled it opened. I leaped backwards and raised my rifle to fire. The second I recognized what it was, I broke into laughter. Hanging in the closet were about a dozen black tuxedos and top hats. My partner grabbed one off a hanger and darted out into the hallway, shouting for the others. His tone hinted at amusement. He led the others into the room and commenced handing out tuxedos and top hats. Each of us put one on over our coats and jammed the hats on top of our helmets. Now we were the best dressed combat engineers in Germany. We split up again and continued to search the first floor. Our progress was slow and tedious. My partner and I shouted to the others that we were finished here and were proceeding to the second floor. They acknowledged our shouts. My heart rate picked up as we bounced up the tile lined stairway, taking the steps two at a time. For a moment I leaned against the hallway wall panting, as I readied myself to enter the next apartment.

I heard movement and noise emanating from a room at the end of the hall. I whispered to my partner to head toward the last door. He made his approach on one side of the hall, hugging close to the wall, while I approached on the other. We moved quietly, uncertain of what was up ahead. As we reached the open door, a powerful looking German soldier with a sadistic smirk jumped into the doorway, startling us. His rifle was aimed directly at my partner's chest. He ducked and somehow tripped me, knocking me down. The German fired and missed. The bullet slammed into the wall behind us as the sound of splintering wood echoed through the hall. My partner leaped on the German, knocking him to the floor. The German grunted in pain but regained his footing first. Standing on his knees, my partner grabbed both of the Germans legs trying to topple him. The German pulled a bayonet from a sheath on his belt and swung it at my partner's head. My partner jerked backwards, the bayonet just missing. The German smashed his knee into my partner's face, knocking him over. All this time, I had been standing poised in the doorway, my feet planted firmly on the floor, waiting for a clear shot. This was it! With my rifle raised hip high, I fired two shots in rapid succession, hitting the German square in the chest. He flinched but didn't go down. Dropping his bayonet, he just stood there a moment, turned towards me and stared. He had a look of disbelief on his face. His right hand moved slowly towards small scarlet holes that were becoming rapidly more visible in the middle of his coat.

His face contorted and his eyes widened and watered. He seemed to be struggling for breath and made gurgling sounds. He staggered and lurched forward, collapsing like a puppet whose strings had been cut. Within a few seconds, an all too familiar odor told me he was dead. He lay there, mouth opened, eyes glazed over, blood pooling under him. The shots had brought heavy foot-steps pounding up the stairs. It was the others from our group. They stopped and stared at the body, their faces devoid of expression. One went over to check the life-less mass and nudged it with his boot, while another asked if we were okay. I averted his gaze and nodded yes. He raised his eyebrows skeptically as he brushed past me. I wiped the sweat from my face with my coat sleeve. It had all happened so fast, that it didn't seem real. My ears were still ringing from the rifle shots, and the rush of adrenaline had left my legs shaking. My part-ner's face was red and puffy, but otherwise, he was all right. He clapped me on the back in a gesture of grati-tude. We all took a minute to compose ourselves, then continued to flush the building as one group. We made our way to the fifth floor. Entering the first door, I saw a grand piano in the middle of the room. I walked over to the piano bench, sat down and stared at the keys. I looked at my partner. A gleam of mischief showed in his eyes. He shouted, "Clear the room!" as he took out his grenade launcher, attaching it to the muzzle of his rifle. I scrambled for cover. Locking a grenade on, he shouted, "Lets shove this fuckin' piano out the window!" He pulled the trigger, hitting the wall next to the window. The muzzle flash momentarily lit the room. A shock wave pulsated through my body, as the thunderous explosion was magnified by the confines of the room. As the smoke cleared, I could see a gaping hole where a wall once stood. I shook my head in disbelief. Already dressed in tuxedos, we were ready for our special concert and proceeded to push the piano out of the opening. From the fifth floor, we heard a crumbling thud, followed by a lot of flat sounding notes. I looked over the edge and whistled under my breath. Suddenly it hit me. We had neglected to see if anyone was down below! All we could do now was hope there wasn't. Well, at least we got some of our frustrations out. Before leaving the building, we perused through some of the rooms on a souvenir hunt. Besides the book I already had under my coat, I picked up a silver spoon, knife, flag and Luger pistol.

It was six thirty in the morning and twelve of us were stopping off at headquarters, after being on patrol all night on the enemy side of the Rhine River. I couldn't wait to take a hot shower, eat and go to sleep. A sergeant was walking toward us with a clipboard and pen in his hand and said, "I need two volunteers to ride shotgun to Maastricht, Holland." He pointed to me and another man and in a firm, crisp tone said, "Both of you just volunteered." Only the army gives choices like these! Minutes later, we were climbing into a six by six truck with a fresh driver already in it. A machine gun would not be necessary for this trip because we were heading sixty five miles southwest, into secured territory. At Maastricht, there was a supply depot. We were picking up extra base plates that would be needed for the construction of a bridge at Dusseldorf. So here I am, exhausted, dirty and hungry, sitting in the front seat of an uncomfortable, hot, bouncing truck, wedged between the driver and my partner. My partner and I were holding our rifles between our legs, butt down, barrel up, using them as supports to keep us propped up in our seats. Our heads bobbed up and down as we tried desperately, but unsuccessfully, to fight off sleep. The next time I opened my eyes, four hours had passed, and we had arrived at the supply depot. The driver told us we kept leaning against him and he was constantly pushing us upright so he could drive. My back and arms were sore as hell from bouncing around and trying to hang on to my rifle. Luckily, my M1 rifle never went off accidentally. The soldiers at the depot already had the base plates ready and waiting for us. It only took them ten minutes to load the truck. There was barely enough time for us to go to the latrine before we had to start heading back. I was hoping we would at least be able to get some decent food. No such luck! At least the driver remembered to pick up a bag of sandwiches from the mess hall before we left. He pulled one out and handed it to me. I nodded a thanks and took several big bites, gulping the sandwich down in seconds. I washed it down with a swig from my canteen. Moments later, I let out a loud, long belch that seemed to shake the truck. We were all such classy guys back then.

Thank God we weren't in enemy territory and it was an uneventful trip, because my partner and I slept through most of the one hundred thirty miles. It was already dark by the time we reached headquarters. The parts would be brought over to the bridge site first thing in the morning. My body ached from head to toe. I was starving, but I wasn't sleepy anymore. I wondered what new thrill would be in store for me tomorrow, here in paradise.

The 1285th and the 1288th Engineer Battalions had already started building the pontoon Bailey bridge across the Rhine River at Dusseldorf. Random sniper fire from the east bank of the river was a constant and present danger. To compound that, the water was rough and chilly, with a strong cold wind blowing down the river from the north. The sunlight glistened in shapeless patches on the surface of the water. The reflection was so bright I was continuously squinting. A pair of sunglasses would have helped right about now, especially the way my head was throbbing. I felt as if I were coming down with a cold or something, and was constantly swiping at my runny noise. This put me in a really foul mood. We were busier than flies on a turd when bullets started splattering in the water all around us. There were already enough hazardous obstacles out here without someone firing at us. Suddenly, an enemy shell burst wide of the span. I wheeled around and dropped prone, covering my ears. My heart pounded and pain shot through my head. Another shell came sailing in, my eyes locked on it as I calculated its trajectory, praying it would miss its target. Seconds later, it plunged harmlessly past me into the water. I lay there a moment forcing my breathing back to normal. The pain in my head eased. I had had it! It was time to retaliate and call in artillery support. Five minutes later I heard the unmistakable drone of tanks as they lumbered along in the distance. I could see the huge brown dust cloud kicked up by their treads. Back lit by the morning sun, ten tanks pulled up onto the sheer rock and earth wall that rose up from the river. They sat side by side, turrets rotating, cannons raised and ready. Wham! Wham! Wham! The tanks started their barrage. Sputtering machine guns could be heard between the rumble of the tanks' cannons. Gaping holes were being gouged out of the east bank along the forest that ridged the north side. The enemy guns went silent, vanishing in a pillar of smoke that pearled up into the sky. After three minutes of intense shelling, the tanks ceased fire. To ensure security, seventeen of us, fully armed, took eight of the motor boats that were used for building the bridge, and went across the river. There wasn't going to be any more sniper fire!

It took about a week to complete the bridge. We spent one whole day just patching bullet holes in the pontoons, using tar and metal plates, hammering in a couple of nails to hold the plates in place. We sealed the holes from the outside. Nobody in my company was injured or killed, as far as I knew, and we were out there every day. One thousand five hundred six feet was the final length of the bridge. It was named after Ernie Pyle. Ernie Pyle was a war correspondent. Pyle, more than any other writer, told the story of the common G.I. Pyle was killed April of 1945, by Japanese machine gun fire on the island of Iwo Jima.

The Germans used frogmen to sabotage and destroy our bridges. In one incident, they had cut loose a loaded coal barge and sent it floating downstream. It slammed into the Ernie Pyle bridge. The damage was so severe that part of the bridge required rebuilding. Patrols were sent upstream to demolish anything that floated which could be a threat to the bridges.

Street Fighting

Ernie Pyle Bridge

Chapter 25
Rheinhausen / Wesel

Fifteen miles north, up the Rhine River, was the City of Rheinhausen, and the location of the 1285th next bridge building assignment. The bridge would link Rheinhausen with Duisburg on the east bank of the Rhine River, not far from the remains of the Adolf Hitler Bridge. Company B would use eleven thousands pounds of explosives to clear the two hundred foot by one hundred fifty foot wide slip at Rheinhausen. At the time the bridge was started, we had no idea that we would achieve a remarkable feat of bridge building. At one thousand five hundred thirty four feet, it was the longest floating Bailey bridge ever built in the world. It would take over five decades before a longer bridge was finally built. (This took place in Bosnia.) It was named the Gerow Bridge, after General Leonard T. Gerow, commander of the fifteenth Army. It was later renamed the Triumph Bridge.

When I finished for the day, I stopped off at headquarters to check the bulletin board to see if I recognized any names on the Z.I. list. This stood for zone of interior. If a soldier were badly wounded, he was sent home. There was also the deceased list. When I saw a name I knew, I felt angry, and muttered to myself, "Shit! Another guy."

It was time to move toward our next bridge building location, the city of Wesel. First, we had to make our way through the cities of Oberhausen, Geldern and Mors.

Our forces were crossing the Rhine River, north of the Ruhr Valley. Wesel, Germany was now the focal point of our troops. When I saw Wesel, it was a mere mud hole after the obliterating, large scale bombing attacks by the American air force. These bombings were quickly followed up by a vast airborne invasion of forty thousand troops east of the Rhine, near the city of Wesel. This was the largest operation of its kind for that time. Day after day, more German civilians found the war taking place in their own backyards. The night sky glowed orange as their country burned to the ground, one city at a time.

A railroad trestle bridge was thrown across the Rhine River in just ten days, although construction plans showed it would take two weeks. It was erected with metal girders made in Luxembourg and wooden piles cut from a German forest. It immediately sped supplies to our forces sweeping across Germany. The decision to use rock, gravel and earth in the construction turned out to be a big mistake. Heavy traffic resulted in major problems and a rebuilding of the bridge was necessary.

At this point in the war, some seventy five thousand United States Army Engineers were at work on sixty three bridges all up and down vital waterways.

When I wasn't helping to build a bridge, I was out setting up temporary water supply stations, loaned out somewhere, on patrol, or fighting a battle. The army always managed to keep me busy!

The large City of Essen was in the industrial Ruhr region, twenty five miles southeast of us, on the east side of the Rhine River. This was where a major battle was brewing, and we were headed there at full speed.

Gerow Bridge

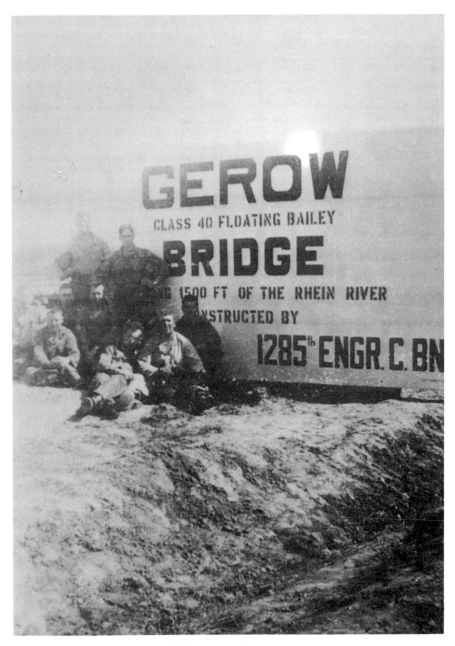

Our Sign

Chapter 26
The Ruhr

The early morning fog had just burned off when we found ourselves twelve miles southeast of Essen, near the City of Wetter, and in the middle of an obscene, bloody battle. Two hundred forty thousand men, or seventeen American divisions, were exerting immense pressure on the Germans. Our soldiers and tanks plunged forward with incredible speed and power, pushing deeper into the region. Men were falling left and right, bodies dotting the fields everywhere. There were no more German antiaircraft, so American planes rained devastation on towns and communications. We were in hot pursuit of the enemy. The smell of death filled the air. My pace quickened. I was moving over the bodies of dead German soldiers. The Germans no longer had an organized army. They were a disintegrating force in chaos, and powerless to stop our advance. With the precision of a surgeon, the Germans were pushed into small pockets, encircled and cut into fragments. They were a stubborn, die-hard army on the retreat, fighting to the point of annihilation. We had already chased, cornered and liquidated thousands, and still they held out. All of a sudden, enemy soldiers started surrendering. In our push forward, a few of the guys around me shot some soldiers trying to surrender. One was knocked clear off his feet and cartwheeled backwards. More and more German soldiers threw down their weapons and raised their hands high above their heads. Some waved white handkerchiefs. I personally captured a group of soldiers. Finally, their General foresaw the impending doom and surrendered them all. It was over and he knew it! He didn't want to see anymore of his men needlessly killed.

The bag of prisoners was enormous. Some three hundred thousand were taken in one mass surrender, while those who preferred to fight on were being exterminated. Many high ranking Nazis were also captured. Since the German army had deserted the town, not many buildings needed to be searched. It would make the mop up job much easier. Distracted a moment, I glanced around. The ditches on both sides of the road were filled with every kind of weapon imaginable. The sheer quantity astonished me. Dazed civilians were wandering aimlessly through the devastated streets. Enemy dead lined the roadside. Dried blood and debris covered their faces. There were bodies without heads or limbs. It had the look and stench of a slaughterhouse. I shut my eyes and graphic pictures flashed in my mind. I quickly opened them again and looked up at the sky. I let the images pass with the gentle breeze that was blowing over the land.

Camps were being set up to hold the prisoners. Because of the large number of men, coils of barbed wire were used to make compounds. Hundreds of tents were being brought in to house them. Most of their equipment had been lost or destroyed during the battle. With their hands behind their heads, the prisoners were herded to the compound. They were beaten, shattered men. Their faces pale and drawn, shoulders slumped, eyes staring down at the ground. Some were limping, some bleeding, some cowering. This had been a bitter blow to them and their war machine. Most of their factories and many of their cities had been totally destroyed. Before the prisoners were placed in the compounds, their documents were checked. Upon examination of the documents, some of the soldiers would be taken to headquarters for interrogation. The next problem that arose was the feeding of all these men. The Germans still had some food left in their trucks, but only enough for about one day. They placed their entire stock of provisions into large kettle's and made some sort of stew. We would have to bring in cases of K-rations and C-rations until kitchens could be set up.

Well, my job in this dirty business was over, for now. I came out of it in one piece, physically, anyway. Now, it was on to my next assignment.

Chapter 27
Cousin Charlie

I heard that the wounded soldiers from my battalion were being brought south to the 45th Evacuation Hospital in St. Windel, Germany. Hearing that, I realized my cousin, Charlie Danish, was stationed there as a medic. I hadn't seen him since before the war. I went to my commanding officer and explained the situation, telling him it was my brother. I asked if I could go see him, since this might be my only chance, if one of us should die. If my officer had known it were my cousin and not my brother he would have never let me go. He gave me an uncertain look as he stroked his chin and said, "since we haven't received new orders yet, you can go." He then pulled out maps of the area. Taking a good hard look at them, he filled me in on what was known. Patrols hadn't gone out in that direction yet, so no one knew if there were Germans out there. I would be crossing into no man's land, and over some sort of mountain range. It would be a total of about sixty five miles. I immediately started preparing for the trek. First thing I got were cigars for my cousin. He loved smoking them. Since I didn't smoke, I traded a few packs of cigarettes, which I had from my K-rations, for a few cigars. I put the cigars in a sock and placed them next to my rifle grenades, which I kept in a little rectangular bag that I carried over my shoulder. I packed plenty of C and K-rations and filled my canteen. I picked up a small submachine gun and two loaded magazines, along with two bandoliers full of ammo for my M1. Last, but not least, was a sleeping bag and some extra clothing. I asked a few buddies if they would take me by truck as far as was allowed. It would save me about a thirty mile walk. Two agreed, but didn't tell our commander, just in case he said no. My buddies dropped me off at the point where the map ended and wished me luck. It was a little before noon, the sky was clear and the air was warming. The sun's heat on my jacket felt good. A perfect day in every respect. I would stick to the road as much as possible. It would probably be the safest route. I had to try and avoid encountering civilians, not to mention, the enemy. After hundreds of thousands of civilians were killed in bombing raids, I wasn't taking any chances to see if they were hostile or not. I was making good time and had only spotted a few people. I ducked off the road, so they never saw me. The countryside was hilly, green and beautiful. The distant view of the fields reminded me of a smooth pool table. The land seemed to stretch on forever, broken up only by farms and wooded areas. I had already walked about five miles and decided it was time to take a break. I moved off the road, almost tripping on a rock. This was no time to injure myself. I sat down behind a group of trees. A squirrel ran down the trunk of one of them and scampered off into the underbrush. After taking a deep breath, I gulped water from my canteen and splashed some on my face. I slowly swirled the canteen, gauging how much water was left before capping it again. I didn't want to run out. Two large birds flew overhead, landing in the tree next to me. They began making loud crowing sounds. Maybe they were trying to tell me it was time to move on. Well, I took their advice and headed out again. The sun was going down, which meant it was time to find a place to hole up for the night. I spotted a small grove of trees not far off the road and headed for it. It was as good a place as any. First thing I did was eat. I couldn't start a fire for fear of someone spotting the smoke. I pulled out my sleeping bag, propped it against the tree and made myself comfortable. Since I was out here by myself, I was taking no chances. I would sleep sitting up with my submachine gun in hand, ready to fire, just in case someone passed by. I figured I had traveled about ten miles this first day. If I could keep up that pace, I'd be there in three days or less. I was completely spent. The sooner I got to sleep, the earlier I could wake and move out again. The air was calm under the full moon as my eyes slowly closed.

I was up at the break of dawn and ready to move out. I had gotten a good night's rest. In fact, it was so quiet out here, I had slept like a baby. The air was moist and the sky looked foreboding. The sun had risen, but was hidden by huge, black puffy clouds. There was a flash of light in the distant sky. A clap of thunder tore through the silence. But luck was with me. It never did start raining. Shafts of sunlight finally broke through, burning off the haze and blanketing the countryside with its warmth. I sure could go for a cup of hot coffee right about now.

I made my way past a large farmhouse. Gray smoke curled and drifted from its chimney. A few hundred yards further I came to a crossroad. As I stood there looking in all directions, I could hear a faint, low hum of what sounded like a rapidly approaching truck. It could be friend or foe. I dashed off the road and hid behind a large outcrop of rock, where I would be able to see them first. I pulled back the bolt on my submachine gun and yanked out a hand grenade, ready for the worst. The truck came into view. There was a large red cross painted on it. As it grew closer, I was able to read 45th evacuation hospital on the bumper. A rush of relief came over me as I leaped up onto the road, waving down the truck. The driver hit the brakes hard, skidding to a stop. The guy was alone and looked very surprised to see someone standing out here, armed to the teeth. He was a large man with a round face. The muscles and veins were prominent in his arms, and beads of sweat showed on his upper lip. I asked him if he were heading to the hospital and if he knew a medic named Charles Danish. The answer to both was yes. He told me to hop in and he would bring me there. He said that the hospital and living quarters were in a college at St.Windell, and that we were only about four miles away. As we crested the last hill, the driver pointed out the valley down below and said that this was St.Windell. The view was breathtaking. He drove me right to the main building. I got out and thanked him for the lift. As he drove off, he waved and asked me to say hello to Charlie for him. I walked into the building and identified myself, stating that I was look-ing for my brother Charles Danish. Someone was imme-diately dispatched to find him. A few minutes later there he was. He grabbed me and gave me a big hug. Boy, was he surprised to see me. His brother! We went back to his room so I could clean up. It had been almost three days since I had last washed or changed my clothing.

His room was a large one that he shared with one other man. We talked a few minutes to catch up on old times. Then I went and took a hot shower. Charlie gave my dirty clothes to a German woman who did the wash there. Once I was all clean and shaved, we headed over to the mess hall which was in the building next door. It was cafeteria style and I had two helpings of scrambled eggs, bacon, toast and coffee. That was a great meal! I could get accustomed to this kind of food in a hurry. I gave my cousin the cigars I had brought. His face lit up in a smile. He thanked me, immediately took out a knife, cut one end open and said, "let's go outside for a smoke." After striking a match, he cupped his hands around the end of the cigar and began taking large puffs while rolling it in his mouth, making sure it was evenly lit. Charlie spent the rest of the day introducing me to people and showing me around.

I spent the next two days in the wards, visiting some of the wounded guys from my outfit while Charlie worked. The ward had the pungent odor of disinfectant. Men lie moaning as nurses scurried in every direction. One soldier was secured in his bed with cloth straps. He lay there looking up, mindlessly muttering to himself. I shuddered as a chill ran through my body. Some of the guys were shot up pretty badly, many had pneumonia. In all probability they would be Z.I.ed. The rest would be picked up in a few days and brought back to their outfits. I had been here three days when trucks from my outfit began arriving. The road back was secure now. Patrols had cleared the way through the no man's area. I would be hitching a ride back with one of the trucks and returning to headquarters. It sure beats walking. I packed my things, said my good-byes and told my cousin I would see him when we got home. An hour later, I was in a truck and on my way.

Once back, we were split up into small groups again, given maps and assigned to set up temporary water supply stations all over the countryside. On May 8, 1945, Germany surrendered, ending the war in Europe. Shortly after, my battalion, the 1285th, was relieved of all tactical assignments. We were one of the hottest and most prolific Combat Engineer Battalions in Europe, and moving to a city in southern Germany for redeployment to the Pacific theater. Ernie Pyle, the war correspondent, said it best, "We were the unknown, unnamed engneers, that had fought so valiantly."

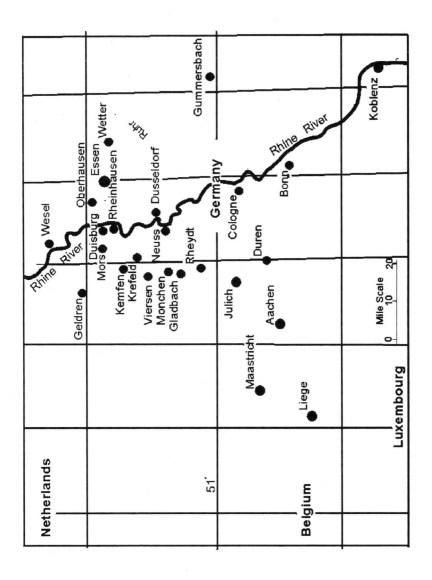

Map

All Cleaned Up

Charlie and Me

Chapter 28
Arles / Marseilles

As we headed south through Germany, we were met by sporadic skirmishes from isolated pockets of Germans, who had no idea the war was over. This meant no rest for the weary. We would have to proceed with extreme caution.

Orders came down from headquarters to pack everything and form a convoy. Our destination was a staging area in southern France. It was located in Arles, fifty miles outside the port city of Marseilles. This would be a five day, four hundred fifty mile trek through France, with one hundred thirty vehicles.

Sixty miles into France we reached Nancy, the first large city. The next city was Dijon, then Lyons and finally the Arles staging area. The only thing I knew about Arles was that Vincent Van Gogh had painted a picture here.

There were tents as far as my eyes could see. It looked as if a boon town had sprung up in the middle of a blistering hot, windy desert. I wondered what jerk picked this location. This overcrowded tent city was home for some one hundred thousand American combat veterans. Close quarters frayed our nerves as the days crept by. The scorching wind was always blowing sand and dust. It managed to get into and on everything. Lines of sand would literally form on the seams of our clothing where perspiration had seeped through. Sometimes we wore handkerchiefs over our faces to keep the grit out of our mouths and nostrils.

Germans prisoners were working in our kitchens and grubbed any extra food they could. They all carried a little tin cup with a spoon attached with a wire. Anything we threw in the garbage, they grabbed and gobbled up. These were the invincible "supermen" of Germany. Now they were learning to eat humble pie. If they ate any good food before it was thrown away, they were sent back to the prison camp. We never worried about their escaping. It was the last thing they wanted to do. The French would kill them if they caught them outside our camp.

My company was lucky. We still had our trucks so we could maneuver around on our own and visit the surrounding areas. Marseilles was only fifty miles away and we headed there to spend some time. It wasn't a very safe place. Army M.P.'s (military police) filled the streets. The place was full of gangsters, prostitutes, bars and soldiers from every nation. There were whole streets where the buildings had been painted yellow. That meant it was dangerous and off limits to American soldiers. The army had set up an area on a beach thirty miles from Marseilles and called it Coney Island. They issued everyone coupons that entitled the holder to two hot dogs and a coke, free of charge. Then, we went swimming in the beautiful, cool, blue Mediterranean Sea.

There was only one time I faced trouble in Marseilles. It was on a trip to pick up new equipment and supplies. We had filled the back of a truck with a pile of loose combat boots held together in pairs by their laces. As we drove slowly through the city on our way back, a group of soldiers from who knows what nation tried to reach in over the tailgate and steal the boots. It almost cost them their lives. We grabbed our rifles and fired over their heads, just missing them. Hell, I didn't want to shoot at allies, but I wasn't going to let them steal our equipment either.

After being here about two weeks, the army took our trucks away and we were stuck in tent city just like everyone else, although most days vehicles were provided to take us swimming. Our trucks would be put on ships that were going to the Philippines. They would be waiting there for us for the invasion of Japan. A lot of the souvenirs I had picked up in Dusseldorf were packed up and on my truck. Unfortunately, when it got to the Philippines someone found them and took them. A lot of time was being spent packing our equipment in crates. Little by little, it was brought down to the port in Marseilles and loaded on lighters, which are small raft- like boats used in

shallow harbors, and then brought out to the ships an-
chored in deeper water. Large cranes were used to load
everything on board, trucks and all.

Everyone was upset about having to go to Japan
to fight another war after just winning one in Europe,
somehow managing to come through it alive and in one
piece. It just wasn't right! The army had plenty of men
available and closer to Japan than we were. It didn't
make sense. We felt exploited and angry, but all we
could do was wait and go where we were told. The army
said we were being sent because we were seasoned,
battle tested, and combat ready, and this would help
shorten the war by six months. This was preposterous.
To protest the army's decision, we mockingly practiced
surrendering. Whenever a high ranking officer came our
way, we marched passed him with our eyes looking down
and our hands clasped behind our heads, as if we were
prisoners.

We knew very little about the war in the Pacific.
Information was limited and censored. Then we started
hearing things that made a bad situation worse. Wild rumors about what to expect in Japan were spreading
through the camp like a fire. Fighting to the death and
military suicide missions! This was incomprehensible to
us. Everyone had listened with trepidation. The Germans had fought bravely, but even they knew when to
quit. Surrendering was the sensible thing to do. I had a
bad feeling about this. It made my stomach queasy. It
was just inconceivable to me that a sane man would plan

his own death. There was also a saying going around camp. "Golden Gate in 48." It meant that the war probably wouldn't be over until 1948 and we wouldn't see the Golden Gate Bridge until then.

Finally, after being here almost a month, we finished packing the last of our new equipment and personal gear. That afternoon, trucks came to ride us over to the port of Marseilles and let us off at the docks to board a troop transport that would take us to the Philippines. This was one hell of a way to see the world.

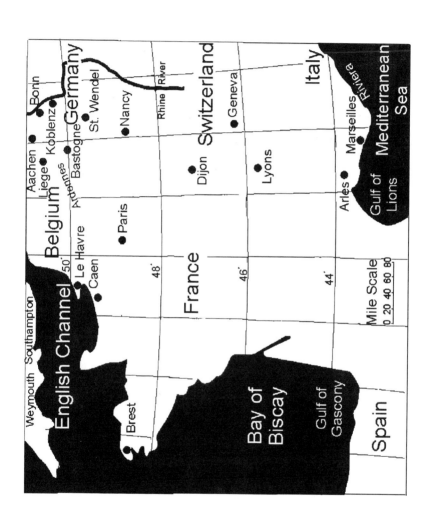

Map

My Platoon - S4 Section: I'm front row, second from left.

Chapter 29
On Our Way

The sky was bright and clear, the air hot and still. My shirt was already soaked with sweat as I stood in line waiting to board a navy troop transport ship. It was a huge ship named the J.C. Breckenridge, fresh out of the shipyards of Carney, New Jersey, and on its maiden voyage. I think it was named after some Civil War general. As I boarded, an officer chalked the front of my helmet with the number 72. I was the 72nd soldier to board. The ship had the smell of a new car. There was a blower system (not air conditioning) that allowed air to move through the entire ship. Everything was so modern and sparkling clean, we could have eaten off the floors. Speaking of eating, my group drew K.P. duty the first day out. Just my luck! Well, at least I didn't have to wait in line to eat, and unlike the tent city, this ship had an abundant supply of provisions.

The trip would take about a month to complete. First, we would sail through the Mediterranean Sea, past the Strait of Gibraltar and into the Atlantic Ocean. From there, the ship would head for the Panama Canal and into the Pacific Ocean. Our destination from there was Manila, in the Philippines. A large staging area located there already had all of our equipment waiting for us. From that point, it was the invasion of Japan.

Before we had left Marseilles, there were unsubstantiated rumors about something big happening in Japan, but no one knew what. On **August 15, 1945**, the ship had already traveled about fifteen hundred miles and was one half day out of the Gibraltar Strait when the speaker system came on. In a loud, joyful voice the transport officer of the vessel bellowed, "Now here this! Now here this! The war is over! We have received official word that our new destination will be New York." It took a whole second of silence for it to penetrate our stunned brains, and then all hell broke loose. I never heard anything like it in my life. It was pure pandemonium. The uproar of cheers, shouts and screams was unimaginable. An indescribable feeling of relief filled the air. Men went wild with joy, throwing all kinds of equipment overboard, whatever they could get their hands on. There was a trail of floating debris forming behind us, including a twelve man life raft. We wouldn't need these things any more. Suddenly, my mind filled with mixed emotions and my bottom lip started to tremble. As the elated cheering slowly diminished, I sank to my knees, eyes filling with tears. The tears flowed down my face and I sobbed like a baby. It was the first time during the entire campaign I had broken down and cried. I thanked God, that "the kill or be killed was over". I was finally going home.

From that time on, the voyage resembled a vacation cruise. We got three meals a day instead of the two which was customary aboard a troopship. Movies were shown every night, and morale was the highest I had ever seen.

Our destination was Pier 88, New York, the main docking area for returning troop ships. Since our mail had been censored, I thought my homecoming would be a big surprise. What I didn't know was that the New York Times printed a list of all the troops by their outfit number, along with the ship they would be on. My sister patiently searched the newspaper every day and when she spotted my outfit number and read that the ship was coming into New York Harbor, she called everyone in the family.

Friday, August 24, 1945, was a bleak, miserable morning with a menacing sky. None of this affected our mood that day. Everyone was up on the ship's deck to see this miracle of really having made it back. The ship had a ten degree list from five thousand of us being on one side of the ship. As we passed near Coney Island ammusement park, I could make out the outline of a huge hotel called the Half Moon. (This hotel no longer exists.) Next, I spotted the Parachute ride, the tallest structure at Coney Island. As we passed Fort Hamilton, Brooklyn, a boat greeted us with a band playing and actress Marlene Dietrich on deck waving. Fire boats were spraying water into the air. Ships and boats of every description were there to greet us, all tooting their horns or whistles as we made our way up the Hudson River. On shore, a giant sign read, "Welcome Home, Well Done." We hung a sign on the ship made out of a bed sheet that said, "1285th Combat Engineers, Le Harvre, France to Tokyo, Japan, New York". When the Statue of Liberty came into sight, there wasn't a dry eye in the crowd. This crying was different. These were tears of joy.

Our ship pulled adjacent to the pier. Ropes were cast down and the ship was moored to huge metal cleats that were attached to the dock. A gangplank was lowered to the pier and we proceeded to exit the ship. Coffee and donuts were waiting for us as we moved down the pier. We lined up and boarded a ferry that took us across the Hudson River to New Jersey. From there, we marched over to the railroad station which was only a short distance away. A tall, heavy set general with a craggy face and sprinkles of gray in his hair greeted us. He had the commanding presence of a seasoned soldier that had seen it all. He spoke slowly, in a clear, calm, reassuring tone. At the end of his short speech, he announced that the army was treating us to a steak dinner. This was a welcome surprise. We boarded a train for a quick ride to Camp Shanks. This is where the army was preparing us a grilled steak dinner, with all the trimmings, in celebration of our home coming. The aroma enveloped me! I hadn't smelled anything that good in close to a year. I had my steak rare, with a jumbo size baked potato smothered in butter and lots of salt. As I feasted, I had to remember to slow down and take human bites. The steak brought back a memory from Julich, Germany. It was the night someone had mistakenly shot and killed a huge cow thinking it was a German soldier. I smiled and chuckled to myself. For dessert, I had a big bowl of vanilla ice cream, my favorite flavor. This was one of the best tasting meals I ever had in the army. Not just that the food was delicious, it was because I was eating it back in the United States. I leaned back in my chair, closed my eyes and savored the moment. Following the meal, another general sang our praises and made a few more announcements.

We were spending the night here. In the morning, all the men who lived in the New York area would board trains that would take us to Fort Dix, New Jersey, the debarkation point.

Chapter 30
Leave at Last

The processing began at Fort Dix. This meant a lot of obligatory paperwork for everyone. We also turned in all our weapons and equipment, and picked up any clothing, if needed. Perfunctory physicals were given. If anyone had any ailments, this was the time to report it to the army and have it taken care of. I was given all the pay that was owed me, along with my leave papers and a train ticket to Grand Central Station. President Harry S. Truman had extended our recuperation leave to thirty days. I was still entitled to thirty days furlough per year, which I hadn't used. It took about two days before the army had sorted out all the paperwork, but once it was completed, I was on my way home. My first stop was the Bronx, to see my mother, father and sister.

It turns out I was the one who was surprised when I got home. Everyone knew I was coming. My sister told me she had seen my ship sail in. She worked for Shell

Oil Company in Rockefeller Center on the fortieth floor, where she had a view of the river. I still had one surprise to spring on my family; I was getting married as soon as possible. My next stop was my fiancee's house in Washington Heights, Manhattan. Her name was Sydell Kastner. I couldn't call her on the telephone because her family didn't have one. (Not everyone had telephones back then.) When I arrived at her apartment door, Sydell was the one who answered. She was a sight for sore eyes. I caught her as she leaped into my arms, hugging and kissing me, tears of joy in her eyes. She also knew I was coming home, but didn't know what day I would show up at her house. She showed me the World Telegram newspaper she had saved from August 24th. The front page headline was about the ship I had come home on, along with a list of companies aboard. We went into the living room and announced to her family that I had a thirty day leave and we wanted to get married as soon as possible. They agreed and immediately started making arrangements. The date was set for Saturday night, September 1, 1945. It was already Friday, August 31st, and a Labor Day weekend on top of that. This was really pushing it. Sydell and I needed to get moving, and fast. We still had to get blood tests and a judge to sign a waiver on the ten day waiting period. Somehow, we managed to pull it all off in twenty four hours. Saturday night we were married in a synagogue in Washington Heights. The ceremony was followed by a party at my mother-in-law's house.

The wedding had gone off without a hitch. Considering the amount of time we had, this was pretty astonishing. Unfortunately, I can't say the same about the honeymoon, at least the start of it. Because of the time restraints and hectic schedule, along with the fact that it was Labor Day weekend, getting a reservation in a hotel in Manhattan was nearly impossible. I had called dozens of them without success, but finally found one. I can not recall the name of it, nor do I wish to. It was located around Eighty Sixth Street and Second Avenue, in a predominantly German neighborhood call Yorktown. It was the first time either of us had ever stayed in a hotel. This added to the excitement. I had even gotten my wife a gardenia, her favorite flower. What an experience this turned out to be. This was one of the seediest places I had ever seen, and it smelled like a mildewed dishcloth. The entire floor had to share one bathroom. There was a single exposed light bulb hanging from a wire in the middle of the ceiling, and these were the good points! Needless to say, we only stayed there for that one night. My father-in-law helped me find another place. This time we stayed at a nice place downtown, around Forty Eighth Street and Eighth Avenue, called the Holland Hotel. The second night we stayed here, my wife invited her best friend and her boyfriend to join us for the evening. Somehow we ended up playing a game of strip poker, the guys against the girls. The girls were losing and were down to their underwear. At that point, they suddenly became embarrassed and started pulling bobby pins from their hair instead of the last of their clothing. Well, we all had a good laugh and ended the game. The next day we read in the newspaper that President Truman was extending the recuperation leave an extra fifteen days, making it a total of forty five days off. This was a pleasant and welcome surprise. We took advantage of this and spent the next two weeks by ourselves having a great time sightseeing and enjoying Broadway shows. We ate lunch at a famous delicatessen called the Gaiety. It was located around Forty Sixth Street and Sixth or Seventh Avenue. Like all good things in life, our honeymoon had to come to an end. Before I knew it, forty five days had passed and I had to return to Fort Dix and the day to day rigors of army life.

Our Wedding Picture

Chapter 31
Back Again

Fort Dix, New Jersey was my first stop. From there, I was given train tickets and was headed for Camp Bowie, Texas, near the town of Brownwood. This was the same camp I had received training in before I had gone overseas. That had been over a year ago, although it felt as if it had been a lifetime ago. But here I was, starting regular army life all over again. This also meant K.P. and latrine duty all over again! About ninety five percent of the guys were back. The rest were either sick, injured or had been discharged already.

Time was hanging heavy on our hands. The army was holding us in service, just in case there was trouble overseas. We were some of the best seasoned, combat ready troops they had. This didn't seem very fair considering the army had established a time and point system, and sixty two points were needed to get out. I had already accumulated seventy two points, while men with fifty points had gone home. Was this another army S.N.A.F.U.?

After being here about a week, a tall officer with an athletic build and bushy eyebrows that met in the middle came around looking for a permanent latrine orderly. It was the first time I had ever volunteered for anything. But there was a good reason. It would be the only job I had to do. I would draw no other duties. Not only that, everyday I'd have help, and once I was done, I was finished for the day. The hard part was getting this pigsty into shape. This was a large latrine and hadn't been used for quite a long time. I couldn't believe the mess that had been left behind. There were used razor blades and their paper wrappers, empty toothpaste tubs and soap wrappers cluttering the latrine. Even though it was a large mess, once the latrine had been thoroughly cleaned it would be easy to maintain.

It took me almost a week of hard work to get this place into pristine condition. The long sinks, toilets and urinal troughs were so encrusted with crud, I had to use a mixture of gasoline and scouring powder to get them clean. I made the mirrors and wooden shelves above the sinks shine. I pulled out all the wooden duckboards from the shower stalls and burned them. I was making sure they would never be used again. This would help stop the spread of athlete's foot. Because I was a water supply technician, I had access to chlorine. I put on my galoshes and used it to wash down the huge shower stalls, floors and benches. From now on, I would do this every week. One thing was certain: the latrine never sparkled like this before. It was so clean one could eat off the floor. Passing inspection should be a snap, and I was ready!

The next morning I was positioned in front of the latrine waiting for an inspection officer. The sun was beating down on my face, warming me. An officer came over and barked loudly and crisply "Attention!" Standing tall, I yelled back "Private First Class Danish reporting sir! The latrine is ready for inspection!" It was such a pretty sight. All the toilet seats were in the up position, almost like they were standing at attention along with me. Needless to say, there was no problem. Actually, the officer seemed rather impressed. He had a slight grin on his face as he rubbed his chin thoughtfully. Now that the inspection was completed, I was done for the day. I went back to my barracks, which had already been inspected, and lied down in bed for a well deserved rest.

I developed a daily routine that kept the latrine in tiptop shape, with plenty of volunteers to help. Some of these guys even had sergeant's stripes. The latrine was already so immaculate, that by ten thirty, we had the job finished and the men were free to go for the day. I stayed until the inspection officer came through. I wouldn't let anyone use the toilets until they were inspected. I did hear a few complaints about that, but the men waited anyway. I spent my extra time doing all kinds of things, including going to the P.X. In the evenings, after dinner, I gave the latrine one last quick cleaning, and then headed back to my barracks to wash up. I would put on my dapper dress uniform, go out and hail a taxicab. It was better than waiting for a camp bus. I was on my way to town to spend time at the U. S. O. (United Service Organization). I would spend many a night here passing time listening to music and socializing.

The 1285th Battalion latrine became famous. Everybody at the post knew about it. It was called "Danish's Den, Where the Elite Meet to Sheet." There was a tall, skinny sergeant in our outfit who was an artist, and had drawn three pictures in pencil. One was an insignia crest with "DD" on it, along with a mop and broom crossing at the center of their handles. There was a sketch of a long urinal with lily pads floating in it, and one was of a table in the latrine, loaded with turkey and other foods. I still have these pictures hanging in my house to this day.

Along with my fame came a down side. I was approached by an officer who told me he would like to see the officers' latrine always look as nice as ours. I wasn't happy about this, but I really didn't have a choice. I was stuck with this extra duty. Officers had a separate barracks and latrine, just much smaller. The next morning I took a group of men over to their latrine and we gave it a thorough cleaning. Considering this place was a lot smaller than our latrine, I was surprised to see what a pigsty it was, although, the officers' barracks weren't much better. Well, I had to look at the bright side. There would be no inspection.

One morning we woke to a surprise. After breakfast, our orders were to report to the rifle range. They had to be kidding! Technically, we were supposed to periodically qualify at the range. But how much practice did an outfit of combat veterans need after fighting a war? S.N.A.F.U. again! Besides, we were going home any day now. Every week the bulletin board listed more names scheduled for discharge. When we got to the range it was already packed with soldiers. We stood there looking at each other, bland expressions on our faces, patience wearing thin. As we waited our turn, an idea hit me. I said to everyone in my group "let's all shoot at the same target." Everyone snickered in agreement, and we selected the center target. The rifle I was using was the same one I had throughout the war. It was like an old friend I hadn't seen in a while. The order was given for us to move up to the firing line and commence rapid fire. Seconds later, some two hundred bullets chewed apart the center target, completely destroying it along with the frame. It had an odd appearance just hanging there in pieces. This was one target nobody would be able to plug. All the other targets had Maggie's Drawers flying. The soldiers in the target pit knew something was up. We all lowered our rifles, stepped back and stood there looking straight ahead. The range officers stared at us in bewilderment for what seemed a very long time. One officer had a scowl as he rubbed at his neck and slowly shook his head. His facial muscles twitched and the veins on his neck stood out as he shouted through clenched teeth, "Dismissed"! The range officers weren't happy, but they sure got our message. Luckily, none of us got into trouble.

With only a few months of army life left, and Christmas days away, I had a bit of bad luck. A cyst swelled up at the base of my tail bone, and I ended up in the hospital. I was informed I had a pilonidal cyst. The pain from this was excruciating! It was impossible to find a comfortable position, whether I stood or sat. I had plenty of company and lots of empathy in the ward I was in. Everyone here had either a rectal problem or a pilonidal cyst. The only treatment was to sit in a hot tub of water everyday for a few hours and wait for the cyst to open. There was an unwritten rule here. If someone's cyst started to open, the hot tub of water was theirs. Everyone looked forward to nighttime. That's when they gave us a few ounces of an elixir of terpin hydrate and codeine. No one here felt any pain. It also made walking and talking a real challenge. After a few days of soaking, my cyst finally opened. A doctor squeezed it out and then let it drain. I bore the pain stoically. Several days later, I was still sore but able to resume my regular routine.

It was January, 1946. A new year had turned the corner and a soft white blanket of snow covered the countryside. I was keeping a constant vigil on our bulletin board. My name would be coming up on the discharge schedule any day now. I was walking past headquarters one afternoon, when one of the officers approached me and asked if I were interested in a promotion to corporal. I would earn ten dollars a month more. With so many men leaving, there were now openings. But, there was a catch. I had to give up my latrine orderly job to procure the promotion. It only took me a second to make a decision. It was a firm "no thank you, sir!" I was having a picnic and wasn't about to give it up for a mere ten dollars.

At the end of January, my name finally appeared on the discharge list. I was elated. The next day, I had turned in my rifle and all my equipment. I was leaving for the separation center at Fort Dix, New Jersey, for debriefing. This is where my army life started, and this is where it would finish.

Paperwork, paperwork, and more paperwork. I was astonished and bewildered by the amount of forms I had to fill out and sign. There were medical examinations, insurance lectures about benefits, and instructions on where to go if I had any problems. If needed, clothing was available to complete a uniform. Everyone was entitled to two full sets. I drew my pay and any money owed me, and received a train ticket to get me home. Mustering out pay was made in three installments, one a month. I had to furnish an address for the army to mail the checks. On February 3, 1946, I received my honorable discharge from the Army of the United States. Hours later, I was boarding a train bound for New York. I was finally going home.

Chapter 32
Home Sweet Home

I was starting over again. Civilian life would take a little getting used to. First order of things was to sublet an apartment for my new bride and myself. We needed our own place to live. We found a small apartment in the Bronx, not far from where my mother lived. A short time later, we sublet an apartment with friends in Flatbush, Brooklyn.

Readjustment wasn't automatic. It came slowly. I was trying to forget some of my experiences in the war, but vivid memories kept flashing in my mind. Sometimes the visions came back in waves. Even sleep offered no escape. I had left a trail of dead friends across Europe. I witnessed ordinary men do extraordinary things in extreme circumstances. I had seen suffering and raw courage. It had taken years of gunfire and rivers of blood to end this war. I can only pray that the endless rows of soldiers' headstones, in their eerie silence, will serve as a grim reminder to the insanity of it all.

On a cold November morning in 1948, the first of two sons were born. My wife and I had started our family and moved to a small town in Queens, New York. There, we bought our first house with a four percent, thirty year, G.I. mortgage. Now, here I am fifty years later, enjoying my retirement and my first born has written my story.

EPILOGUE

It had taken almost six years to end World War II, with the Allied forces emerging victoriously. Some sixteen million men and women had worn uniforms. One and three quarter million American soldiers were in combat. Almost three hundred thousand were killed in action. The monetary cost was estimated well over one trillion dollars. The pen had followed the sword with the signing of formal surrender agreements. At last, the world could pause a minute and take a deep breath. The killing and destruction had ceased. But there were other costs that could not be measured. Just because the war had ended, didn't mean the pain had stopped. Lives had been changed irrevocably. Military forces occupied cities. Economies were in shambles. There was only rubble where homes, businesses and churches once stood. Food, clothing and shelter were in short supply for many people. Everyone had suffered equally in their loss of loved ones who once shared this world with us. The continental United States was lucky. Emerging relatively unscathed, we became the sole possessor of the deadliest weapon ever made. Our principles, traditions and fundamental freedoms were still securely in place. I was lucky also. I made it home in one piece. I had kept the faith and somehow survived everything the enemy had thrown at me.

I had served my country a total of three years, one month and six days. For eight months and eighteen days I was fighting overseas. My battalion received a Presidential Citation for the building of the bridges across the Rhine River. We also received a Bronze Battle Star for the Battle of the Ruhr. I received four other decorations. They were the: American Service Medal, World War II Victory Medal, European African Middle Eastern Service Medal and a Good Conduct Medal.

I can only pray that this will be the last war the world will ever see.

ONE SOLDIER'S MEMORIES

ADDENDUM

Four months after this book was published, on the evening of Thursday, March 18, 1999, while resting in his Florida home, Jack Danish suffered a massive heart attack. Never regaining consciousness, he died on Saturday evening, March 20, 1999 with his family at his hospital bedside. We will all miss him dearly. But this old soldier will never die. His memory will live on in the hearts and minds of those who loved him, knew him and read his story. God bless him, may he rest in peace.

July 31, 1923 - March 20, 1999

BIBLIOGRAPHY

Chronicle of the 20th Century Chronicle Publications Incorporated Mount Kisco, New York

Engineering The Victory. The story of The Corps of Engineers, United States Army

Statistics and weapon information were obtained from various Departments of the United States Army

World-Telegram Newspaper August 24, 1945 New York Edition